2/15

OPPOSING VIEWPOINTS® SERIES

The Democratic Party

Other Books of Related Interest:

Opposing Viewpoints Series
Civil Liberties

Congressional Ethics

Dictatorships

Government Spending

At Issue Series
Does the World Hate the US?

Are Government Bailouts Effective?

Negative Campaigning

Should the Federal Income Tax Be Eliminated?

Should the Government Regulate What People Eat?

Current Controversies Series
Politics and Religion

US Government Corruption

Women in Politics

"Congress shall make no law ... abridging the freedom of speech, or of the press."

First Amendment to the US Constitution

The basic foundation of our democracy is the First Amendment guarantee of freedom of expression. The Opposing Viewpoints series is dedicated to the concept of this basic freedom and the idea that it is more important to practice it than to enshrine it.

OPPOSING VIEWPOINTS® SERIES

The Democratic Party

Noah Berlatsky, Book Editor

GREENHAVEN PRESS
A part of Gale, Cengage Learning

GALE
CENGAGE Learning·

Farmington Hills, Mich • San Francisco • New York • Waterville, Maine
Meriden, Conn • Mason, Ohio • Chicago

Elizabeth Des Chenes, *Director, Content Strategy*
Douglas Dentino, *Manager, New Product*

© 2015 Greenhaven Press, a part of Gale, Cengage Learning.

WCN: 01-100-101

Gale and Greenhaven Press are registered trademarks used herein under license.

For more information, contact:
Greenhaven Press
27500 Drake Rd.
Farmington Hills, MI 48331-3535
Or you can visit our Internet site at gale.cengage.com

For product information and technology assistance, contact us at

Gale Customer Support, 1-800-877-4253
For permission to use material from this text or product, submit all requests online at
www.cengage.com/permissions

Further permissions questions can be emailed to permissionrequest@cengage.com

Articles in Greenhaven Press anthologies are often edited for length to meet page requirements. In addition, original titles of these works are changed to clearly present the main thesis and to explicitly indicate the author's opinion. Every effort is made to ensure that Greenhaven Press accurately reflects the original intent of the authors. Every effort has been made to trace the owners of copyrighted material.

Cover Image © Jacob Hamblin/Shutterstock.com.

LIBRARY OF CONGRESS CATALOGING-IN-PUBLICATION DATA

The Democratic Party / Noah Berlatsky, book editor.
     pages cm. -- (Opposing viewpoints) Summary: "Opposing Viewpoints is the leading source for libraries and classrooms in need of current-issue materials. The viewpoints are selected from a wide range of highly respected sources and publications"-- Provided by publisher.
     Includes bibliographical references and index.
     ISBN 978-0-7377-7252-4 (hardback) -- ISBN 978-0-7377-7253-1 (paperback)
     1. Democratic Party (U.S.)--History--Juvenile literature. I. Berlatsky, Noah.
     JK2316.D445 2014
     324.2736--dc23
                                                                          2014021948

Printed in the United States of America
1 2 3 4 5 6 7 18 17 16 15 14

Contents

Chapter 2: How Does the Democratic Party Relate to Important Voting Groups?

Chapter 3: What Are Controversial Domestic Issues Within the Democratic Party?

Chapter 4: What Are Controversial Foreign Policy Issues Within the Democratic Party?

Why Consider Opposing Viewpoints?

"The only way in which a human being can make some approach to knowing the whole of a subject is by hearing what can be said about it by persons of every variety of opinion and studying all modes in which it can be looked at by every character of mind. No wise man ever acquired his wisdom in any mode but this."

John Stuart Mill

In our media-intensive culture it is not difficult to find differing opinions. Thousands of newspapers and magazines and dozens of radio and television talk shows resound with differing points of view. The difficulty lies in deciding which opinion to agree with and which "experts" seem the most credible. The more inundated we become with differing opinions and claims, the more essential it is to hone critical reading and thinking skills to evaluate these ideas. Opposing Viewpoints books address this problem directly by presenting stimulating debates that can be used to enhance and teach these skills. The varied opinions contained in each book examine many different aspects of a single issue. While examining these conveniently edited opposing views, readers can develop critical thinking skills such as the ability to compare and contrast authors' credibility, facts, argumentation styles, use of persuasive techniques, and other stylistic tools. In short, the Opposing Viewpoints Series is an ideal way to attain the higher-level thinking and reading skills so essential in a culture of diverse and contradictory opinions.

In addition to providing a tool for critical thinking, Opposing Viewpoints books challenge readers to question their own strongly held opinions and assumptions. Most people form their opinions on the basis of upbringing, peer pressure, and personal, cultural, or professional bias. By reading carefully balanced opposing views, readers must directly confront new ideas as well as the opinions of those with whom they disagree. This is not to argue simplistically that everyone who reads opposing views will—or should—change his or her opinion. Instead, the series enhances readers' understanding of their own views by encouraging confrontation with opposing ideas. Careful examination of others' views can lead to the readers' understanding of the logical inconsistencies in their own opinions, perspective on why they hold an opinion, and the consideration of the possibility that their opinion requires further evaluation.

Evaluating Other Opinions

To ensure that this type of examination occurs, Opposing Viewpoints books present all types of opinions. Prominent spokespeople on different sides of each issue as well as well-known professionals from many disciplines challenge the reader. An additional goal of the series is to provide a forum for other, less known, or even unpopular viewpoints. The opinion of an ordinary person who has had to make the decision to cut off life support from a terminally ill relative, for example, may be just as valuable and provide just as much insight as a medical ethicist's professional opinion. The editors have two additional purposes in including these less known views. One, the editors encourage readers to respect others' opinions—even when not enhanced by professional credibility. It is only by reading or listening to and objectively evaluating others' ideas that one can determine whether they are worthy of consideration. Two, the inclusion of such viewpoints encourages the important critical thinking skill of objectively evaluating an author's credentials and bias. This evaluation will illuminate an author's reasons for taking a particular stance on an issue and will aid in readers' evaluation of the author's ideas.

It is our hope that these books will give readers a deeper understanding of the issues debated and an appreciation of the complexity of even seemingly simple issues when good and honest people disagree. This awareness is particularly important in a democratic society such as ours in which people enter into public debate to determine the common good. Those with whom one disagrees should not be regarded as enemies but rather as people whose views deserve careful examination and may shed light on one's own.

Thomas Jefferson once said that "difference of opinion leads to inquiry, and inquiry to truth." Jefferson, a broadly educated man, argued that "if a nation expects to be ignorant and free . . . it expects what never was and never will be." As individuals and as a nation, it is imperative that we consider the opinions of others and examine them with skill and discernment. The Opposing Viewpoints series is intended to help readers achieve this goal.

David L. Bender and Bruno Leone,
Founders

Introduction

"As Obama struggles to achieve his second-term domestic agenda, a more liberal and populist voice is emerging within a Democratic Party already looking ahead to the next presidential election. The push from the left represents both a critique of Obama's tenure and a clear challenge to Hillary Rodham Clinton, the party's presumptive presidential front-runner, who carries a more centrist banner."

—*Zachary A. Goldfarb,*
"More Liberal, Populist Movement
Emerging in Democratic Party
Ahead of 2016 Elections,"
Washington Post, *November 30, 2013*

For years, "liberal" was seen as a kind of political slur, and politicians would try desperately to avoid having it applied to them. From the 1960s through the 1980s, "liberal came to mean letting criminals terrorize America's cities, hippies undermine traditional morality, and communists menace the world," wrote Peter Beinart in a February 5, 2014, article in the *Atlantic*. No wonder that in the 1990s, Bill Clinton ran as a centrist, positioning himself against the liberal Democratic establishment.

Recently, however, commenters have pointed out that the Democratic Party is becoming more liberal. In a November 7, 2011, article at Gallup, Frank Newport, Jeffrey M. Jones, and Lydia Saad reported that the number of Democrats who self-identified as liberal increased by two points, from 35 percent to 37 percent, between 2008 and 2011. A January 10, 2014,

Gallup article by Jeffrey M. Jones found that the number of Americans who identify as liberal reached 23 percent in 2014. That is still significantly smaller than the 38 percent of Americans who identify as conservative, but the gap between liberal and conservative identification is smaller than it has been since 1992, when Gallup began tracking identification.

Democratic strategist Steve Rosenthal in a January 16, 2014, op-ed in the *Washington Post* pointed to a number of specific issues on which America is becoming more liberal. Support for marijuana legalization has jumped from 31 percent in 2000 to 58 percent in October 2013. Support for same-sex marriage has increased significantly; in 2013 58 percent of Americans were in favor of marriage rights for gays and lesbians. Support for big business has fallen, and support has risen for Democratic policies on immigration, emphasizing a path to citizenship rather than border security. Rosenthal concludes, "With the knowledge that most Americans are, in fact, behind them, Democrats no longer need to fear running on their beliefs. They should stop letting special interests on the right hold ideas and ideals hostage and start listening to voters."

Other commenters disagree, however. Andrew Kohut in a February 28, 2014, op-ed in the *Washington Post* argues that growing liberal influence in the Democratic Party might damage the party's long-term electoral chances. He notes that liberals do not have as much influence in the Democratic Party as do conservatives in the Republican Party, and he says that "under the more centrist [Barack] Obama administration, the leftward movement of Democratic voters has been of limited political consequence." However, he says, liberals differ in important ways from the rest of the electorate—they tend not to believe that hard work helps people get ahead, they see the deficit as relatively unimportant, and they are relatively unlikely to be religious. Though liberals are not a majority of the Democratic Party, they do make up a large share of primary voters, raising the possibility that liberals could elect a national candidate significantly to the left of the rest of the electorate. This, Kohut says, "might weaken the ideological and demographic coalition that has led the party to victory in four of the past six national elections."

Molly Ball in a February 7, 2014, article in the *Atlantic* agrees that liberals have gained some ground in the Democratic Party, but she says that worries about them controlling the party are overblown. She points out that while conservative activists have repeatedly unseated establishment Republicans in primaries, Democratic liberals have had no such successes. "This dynamic means that compared to Republicans, Democrats are relatively free to antagonize their ideological core supporters," Ball concludes. Even very conservative Democrats, such as Senator Ben Nelson of Nebraska, have not faced liberal primary challenges. Furthermore, while Obama is more liberal than Senate Democrats in many ways, he is probably less liberal than former presidents Bill Clinton, Jimmy Carter, or John F. Kennedy, according to an academic study Ball cites.

Moreover, as of 2014, the perceived front-runner for the 2016 Democratic nomination was not liberal senator Elizabeth Warren, but Hillary Clinton, a mainstream Democrat with longtime ties to the centrist wing of the party. Liberals may be gaining power, but it is unclear how they will translate that power into actual policy changes or leadership anytime soon.

The remainder of this book examines other important issues facing the Democratic Party in chapters titled "What Factors Affect Democratic Electoral Chances?," "How Does the Democratic Party Relate to Important Voting Groups?," "What Are Controversial Domestic Issues Within the Democratic Party?," and "What Are Controversial Foreign Policy Issues Within the Democratic Party?" By presenting viewpoints from many different commenters, this volume seeks to provide an understanding of the Democratic coalition and Democratic policies.

CHAPTER 1

What Factors Affect Democratic Electoral Chances?

Chapter Preface

One of the most important pieces of legislation passed during Democratic president Barack Obama's first term was the Patient Protection and Affordable Care Act (PPACA), also known as Obamacare. The PPACA radically overhauled the nation's health care system with the intention of insuring the uninsured and making health care more affordable. The law was signed in 2010, and most of its major provisions were phased in by 2014.

Though individual portions of the PPACA are very popular, as a whole the law has polled very badly. Since the PPACA was backed by Obama, Republicans have hoped that the unpopularity of the law will damage Democratic chances in the 2016 presidential election, and perhaps even beyond that. There is some evidence that the health care law has already hurt Democrats. For example, Sarah Kliff in a March 8, 2012, article in the *Washington Post* reports that in the 2010 midterm elections, Democrats who had voted for the PPACA did 5.8 points worse than comparable Democrats who had not voted for the bill. That gap was enough to have cost the Democrats dozens of seats, meaning the PPACA may have lost them the House of Representatives in 2010.

On the other hand, some commenters have argued that the PPACA won't necessarily hurt Democratic fortunes. For example, Michael Tomasky in a December 5, 2013, article at the Daily Beast website argues that for most people the PPACA will be "very positive indeed." They will find that "they got insurance, or decent insurance, for the first time in their lives." As a result, he says, the PPACA's popularity will grow and will eventually be a net positive for Democrats who supported it.

Finally, political scientist Jonathan Bernstein argues in a January 21, 2014, post at Bloomberg that the PPACA is unlikely to make much difference to Democrat electoral chances one way or the other. "There's very little evidence that voters total up benefits they've received from government and vote for the party responsible for them," Bernstein says. "Instead, to the (relatively small) extent that voters deviate from partisanship, they're most likely to reward or punish the incumbent party based on how things are going in general, with the economy usually the biggest piece."

The remainder of this chapter examines other factors that may affect Democratic electoral fortunes, including demographic changes, voter ID laws, and immigration reform.

"Mississippi—the deepest of the Deep South states—is on its way to becoming the first majority African-American state."

Red, Redder, Reddest, Blue! Changing Demographics Could Make Mississippi, Texas the Republican Party's Worst Nightmare

R.L. Nave

R.L. Nave is a reporter for the Jackson Free Press. *In the following viewpoint, he argues that growing numbers of black and Latino voters in Mississippi could, in the long term, shift the state to a Democratic majority. An increased number of Latino immigrants in Texas could also move that state toward the Democratic Party. If trends continue, Nave argues, the Deep South could be competitive, rather than solidly Republican, for the first time in at least a generation, and Republicans would be in serious trouble in national elections.*

As you read, consider the following questions:

1. What does Bill Chandler say that Republicans are trying to do to tip elections in states where they exert significant control?

2. Why are African American numbers growing in the South, according to Nave?

3. What was the "Texas Chainsaw Gerrymander," according to the viewpoint?

One day, all of Mississippi will look like Scott County. A largely farming community located in the heart of this conservative Deep South state, Scott County is home to the highest proportion of Latinos in Mississippi, at around 11 percent, who mainly come to work in corporate poultry factories. Combined with the county's roughly 37 percent African-American population (which mirrors the overall black population in Mississippi), blacks and Latinos make up almost half the population there.

So far, Scott County's blacks and Latinos—both Democratic-leaning groups—haven't been able to tip the balance of political power; Mitt Romney, who barely campaigned in the state, won 54 percent of the county's vote in 2012.

And Republicans are doing everything in their power to keep it that way, in Mississippi and in other states where they exert significant control, contends Bill Chandler, executive director of the Mississippi Immigrants Rights Alliance. Chandler points to new requirements for voters to show government-issued identification at the polls in Mississippi and other southern states as well as implementing strict immigration enforcement laws in Alabama and Arizona, which resulted in a Supreme Court case this year.

Conservative whites are extremely concerned that they'll eventually be outnumbered by black and brown voters, Chandler, whose organization investigated claims of vote suppression and led voter-registration drives in Scott County in 2012, told *International Business Times.*

Many Americans, including the leaders of the major political parties, consider the Deep South inconsequential in national elections. Since the 1980s, the region has shifted from almost uniformly Democratic to solidly Republican. Most southern states have Republican governors, legislatures and predominantly Republican congressional delegations with a smattering of racially gerrymandered districts that give blacks one or two seats in key states. As a result, national Republicans rarely visit the South except for perfunctory stops to stump during party primaries and national Democrats rarely bother with wasting the party's money there.

Yet, political analysts say the South could portend the future of the American political system more than any other region of the country. Republican failures to take back the White House in the last two presidential cycles—largely due to the participation of blacks and Latinos in battleground states—have touched off debates within the party about whether it is too white, too conservative, too regionally centered. Largely left out of that debate, yet crucial to it, is that Mississippi—the deepest of the Deep South states—is on its way to becoming the first majority African-American state. And when that happens, if observers such as Chandler are right, Mississippi will go from red to reddest to blue, with not so much as a hint of violet in between. And other states with large minority populations—most of them in the South, most now solidly Republican, most notably conservative powerhouse Texas—won't be far behind.

A Changing Electorate

Blacks make up 37 percent of Mississippi's population, and though Republicans dominate statewide elections, black Democrats wield an extraordinary amount of political influence in the state. Mississippi has the most black elected officials of any other state. Seventeen contiguous western counties, which include the Mississippi delta—the most heavily concentrated slave area in America before the Civil War— already have majority black populations, some with as high as 80 percent.

U.S. Rep. Bennie Thompson, the congressman who represents the delta and some adjacent hill country (a district gerrymandered to ensure a large black majority, which had the effect of ensuring Republican winners in neighboring, former swing districts that lost their largest blocs of black voters) is one of the longest serving and most powerful blacks on Capitol Hill. In 2011, for the first time in the state's history, an African-American won a major party's gubernatorial nomination, and blacks make up the majority of the Democratic caucus in the state legislature. "We are a long way away, from African-Americans' numbers growing large enough to help elect a Democratic governor or put Mississippi in the win column for a Democratic presidential candidate," Byron D'Andra Orey, a political science professor at Jackson State University, said.

Orey acknowledges that if it's going to happen anywhere, it will happen in the Deep South, and most likely in Mississippi. Already, 57 percent of African-Americans live in the South and their numbers are growing as more blacks move back to the region, reversing a trend known as the Great Migration, from 1910 to 1970, when blacks fled to northern and western cities.

Orey, who studies racial trends in Mississippi elections, said even with their large numbers, black voter turnout in Mississippi rarely matches white voter participation, but he said the migration of Latinos, whose numbers are growing the fastest of any group, could be game changers. Between 2000 and 2010, Latinos increased their numbers in Alabama and Mississippi by 106 percent and 145 percent, respectively, according to the Pew Hispanic Center.

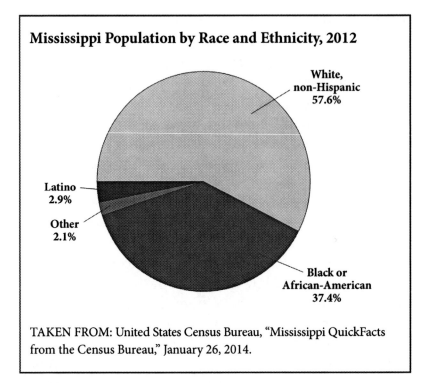

Mississippi Population by Race and Ethnicity, 2012

White, non-Hispanic 57.6%

Latino 2.9%

Other 2.1%

Black or African-American 37.4%

TAKEN FROM: United States Census Bureau, "Mississippi QuickFacts from the Census Bureau," January 26, 2014.

Observers of political trends say the likeliest scenario is Mississippi's population more closely resembling Scott County's, with a 50 percent or so nonwhite population, and then peeling off just enough of the white vote to make the state go from red to blue. Together, blacks, Latinos, and Asians—all of which tend to vote Democratic—barely make up 40 percent of Mississippi's population, yet Barack Obama won close to 45 percent of the state's overall vote.

Then There's Texas

Orey said states such as Texas and Arizona provide the best example of how majority minority populations can spur political change even without holding power. Texas, where non-Hispanic whites, or Anglos, are 44.5 percent of the population, is the nation's second fastest-growing state, having added five million people since 2000, with Latinos accounting for more than two-thirds of the population surge, mostly from western states such as California. The California-Texas emigrants are generally settling in the few Democratic strongholds of Dallas, Houston and Austin, close to jobs and family members. At the same time, the largely white Texas suburbs are exploding in population. Texas is home to eight of the nation's 15 fastest-growing municipalities with at least 50,000 people, U.S. Census Bureau information shows, and of those cities, three are suburbs of Austin.

Despite their large numbers in Texas, Latinos make up only one-third of eligible voters and the state remains safely Republican. Romney won 57 percent of Texas' vote, and the state hasn't elected a Democratic governor since 1990 or sent a Democratic senator to Washington since Lloyd Bentsen won a third term in 1988. And as in Mississippi, the state is getting more overtly conservative as its minority populations increase. Orey said it's no coincidence that where you have a high and growing concentration of blacks and Latinos, you have Republicans increasingly attempting to control the outcome of elections.

"I would make the argument that there's a cause and effect," Orey said.

Battle for the Map

Even Mississippi's former governor, Haley Barbour, who flirted with the idea of running for the GOP nomination for president in 2012, believes his party is in trouble. Following the 2012 campaign, when Obama hammered Romney in all regions except the South—again, due to participation by blacks, Latinos and young people, Barbour said of the GOP, "We've got to give our political organization a very serious proctology exam. . . . We need to look everywhere."

While Republicans are soul-searching, Democrats are beginning to recognize that the South could be in play for them down the road.

On a recent mid-October evening in Jackson, about 75 people gathered for a town hall meeting where U.S. Sen. Bernie Sanders, of Vermont, was scheduled to be the featured speaker. As it turned out, Sanders couldn't attend and participated in the meeting via an Internet camera because that night Congress was set to vote to reopen the federal government after its controversial 16-day shutdown. An Independent who votes with Democrats, Sanders pointed to the shutdown as reason for Democrats to spread the political playing field into conservative southern states. Though it is possible that demographics will ultimately be the driving factor, Sanders told those assembled, "If you don't get involved in the conservative states, they'll never be battleground states."

Sanders' Mississippi appearance was to be one stop on a tour sponsored by South Forward, a Democratic political action committee that aims to recapture statehouses in Dixie as well as, the PAC's executive director Jay Parmley says, redraw the lines that put his party at a severe disadvantage. "We have never before had such lopsided lines for legislative seats. There are very few true swing districts left where either party can win," Parmley told *IBTimes*.

For Democrats, the most valuable prize on that battlefield would be more influence in state legislatures, which oversee redrawing voting maps once per decade. Parmley's view is that partisan redistricting, or gerrymandering, is a key factor in the recent, expensive and debilitating partial government shutdown, which some say jeopardized America's economic status.

Few states provide a better case study for how redistricting can change a political outcome despite its demographics than the Lone Star State and its 2003 redistricting effort led by powerful Republican congressman Tom DeLay. While Texas' population grew enough to warrant giving the state four new congressional districts since 2000 (giving it the nation's largest majority Republican congressional delegation), that redistricting effort elicited harsh criticism of racial gerrymandering.

One of those districts, which came to be called the Fajita Strip, stretched 350 miles between Austin hill country and the Rio Grande delta on the U.S.-Mexico border and was 25 miles wide at its widest point. Eventually, a court ordered the district redrawn because it diluted Hispanic voting strength. The plan, which conservative magazine the *Weekly Standard* termed "the Texas Chainsaw Gerrymander" for the way it slashed Democratic power—and by extension the power of its most loyal constituencies, Latinos and blacks—wasn't the first time a voting map was so unapologetically manipulated to ensure electoral success for a political party; in blue states, Democrats have strong-armed redistricting the same way. In fact, if they get a shot, Democrats have vowed to do the same thing all over the South.

Parmley, the South Forward leader, said, "It'll take a few election cycles, but districts that were drawn to be very safely Republican, just because of demographic shifts, will become more competitive. Then the question becomes how many legislative seats do we win in 2020, so when we redraw the lines in 2022, they're more structurally advantageous for us."

Texas may be laying the groundwork for such a shift. Democratic state senator Wendy Davis, whose political celebrity is on the ascent since she filibustered a controversial abortion bill and announced she would seek the governorship, has both parties wondering aloud if Latinos, a few blacks and progressive transplants to major urban centers can swing the state Democratic.

If that could happen in the state that George W. Bush and Rick Perry hail from, it could happen anywhere.

> "Through intermarriage, Latinos and
> Asian Americans are becoming simi-
> larly mainstreamed. Indeed, in politics,
> business, and culture, it's not hard to
> find examples of 'minorities' who are
> indistinguishable from whites."

Changing Demographics Will Not Necessarily Benefit Democrats

Jamelle Bouie

*Jamelle Bouie is a staff writer for the Daily Beast and a former
fellow at the* American Prospect *and the Nation Institute. In the
following viewpoint, he argues that growing numbers of Asian
Americans and Hispanic Americans in the United States will not
necessarily give the Democratic Party an inevitable advantage.
He acknowledges that at the moment these groups vote overwhelmingly for Democrats and that their numbers are growing.
He points out, however, that immigrants or minority groups in
the past, such as Italian Americans and Irish Americans, eventually assimilated, saw themselves as white, and began to vote with*

the white majority. If that history is repeated, he says, Asian American and Hispanic American voting patterns may change, and the Republican Party may get a new bloc of voters.

As you read, consider the following questions:

1. What was the "Myth of Mobilization," and why do Galston and Kamarck say that myth has become a reality?

2. According to Bouie, why did "formerly stalwart" Irish and Italian Democrats shift to Republicans?

3. What does Bouie say that Republicans could do to permanently alienate minority voters?

By 2050, the U.S. population is expected to increase by 117 million people, and the vast majority of that increase—82 percent—will be immigrants or the children of immigrants. By all accounts, the United States will be a "majority-minority" country, with white Americans as a large plurality, supplanted by a Latino, African-American, and Asian-American majority.

Growing Democratic Strength

It's something to keep in mind as we watch the present-day Republican Party crash on the rocks of a failed fight against the Affordable Care Act (ACA) [officially known as the Patient Protection and Affordable Care Act, or Obamacare], the health-care reform law that will deliver a large share of its benefits to minorities and others who just a few decades ago were a small share of the American electorate. Indeed, this fight—a last-ditch effort against the signature legislation of an ascendant coalition—is emblematic of the trends explained by William Galston and Elaine Kamarck in their recent *Democracy* essay ["The New Politics of Evasion." Issue #30]. The GOP's rearguard action against the ACA highlights the demographic problems that come with the Republicans' alienation from Latinos, Asian Americans, and young working-class whites, and underscores the party's failure to grapple with the income inequality, stagnation, and middle-class retrenchment that define this economic era.

Galston and Kamarck's analysis of the GOP's challenging future is preceded by a re-evaluation of their landmark 1989 essay on the prospects for Democrats in the wake of Michael Dukakis's devastating defeat [in the 1988 presidential election]. In that essay, they diagnosed a broken party alienated from the American mainstream and they rallied a generation of reformers, their allies in elected office, and eventually their standard-bearer in the White House. The Democratic Party of today, the one that prevailed in three of the last four national elections (2006, 2008, and 2012) and won a majority of the popular vote in two consecutive presidential contests (and at least a plurality in five of the last six), is a far cry from the one that nominated Dukakis. It's now a broad, national party that wins public support on most core issues of American governance.

But in looking at the future of the party—and its impressive demographic advantage—there is a note of inevitability in Galston and Kamarck's recent essay that is unwarranted. In their re-exploration of the "Myth of Mobilization"—the idea, tackled in their 1989 essay, that Dukakis could have won with higher minority turnout—they argue, "What was myth in 1981 ... has become reality in 2012. The nonwhite vote as a share of the electorate has expanded significantly, primarily because of disproportionately large increases among mixed-race voters, Asians, and Hispanics."

We saw the consequences of this in the 2012 election, where "Republicans found themselves on the wrong side of a demographic tidal wave." Given the long-term trends—growing Latino immigration and intermarriage between whites and other minority groups—Galston and Kamarck argue that it will only get worse for Republicans: "By the middle of this century ... whites will no longer constitute a majority of our population. In such circumstances, a nearly all-white party, which is what Republicans have become, would have *no chance of obtaining an electoral majority.*" [Emphasis added.]

Galston and Kamarck are quick to acknowledge the other forces at work: namely, a GOP economic agenda that has little to offer the majority of Americans, who don't feel they benefit from deregulation, spending cuts, and upper-income tax cuts. They write that most Americans see "the GOP as a party that favors the rich and opposes every effort to make them shoulder a larger share of the revenue burden." What's more, the Republican Party is out of touch with a growing majority of voters on same-sex marriage, immigration reform, and environmentalism.

Not Inevitable

But that said, their essay seems to overstate the demographic case against the GOP. Yes, for the short term, demographics pose a huge hurdle to the Republican Party's national aspirations. If the 2016 election looks anything like the ones in 2008 and 2012, the Democratic candidate will win overwhelming majorities of Latino, Asian-American, and mixed-race voters, with near unanimous support from African Americans. And if the nominee is former secretary of state Hillary Clinton, there's a fair chance the party can improve its margin among white women, who—in recent years—have made a small move away from the Republican Party.

But if we look ahead 40 years, there's a decent chance this Democratic majority never materializes. Ethnic identity is fluid—it shifts and changes with the circumstances of society. Right now, we think of Latinos and Asian Americans as separate from the white mainstream. But there's no guarantee that will be true in the future. Indeed, if it isn't, we could have a politics that looks similar to the one we have now.

In the beginning, there was the Anglo-American majority. The descendants of English subjects, these men and women belonged to a shared culture rooted in the British Isles. Then came German immigrants, who then assimilated into the colonial way of life. Over time, other waves of immigrants would join this "mainstream" and carve a place for themselves. None of this was automatic, and in the case of the Irish, Italians, and Eastern Europeans, it was preceded by a long period of discrimination and prejudice. At the turn of the century, in fact, Italians and Irish were stigmatized groups that could not be brought into the mainstream. They were seen as nearly as separate—as irreducibly *different*—as African Americans were.

But compared to their black compatriots, they had a significant advantage: fair skin. With time, mobility, and distance, they could assimilate and become indistinguishable from the Anglo majority. And so they did. As they rose out of working-class professions and joined a burgeoning middle class, they and other immigrants *became white*. By the middle of the twentieth century, Irish, Italian, and Eastern European Americans weren't as distinct a class as they were at its turn; the shared experience of the Great Depression and sacrifice of the Second World War bound them to the mainstream.

What's key to remember is that this evolution corresponded with a political shift. For almost a century, the Democratic Party was identified with the interests of European immigrants. Irish and Italians formed the foundation of the Democratic machines of the North and Midwest, and were the backbone of the coalition that swept Franklin Roosevelt and his New Dealers into office, then Harry Truman, and later, John F. Kennedy and Lyndon Johnson.

Politics and Assimilation

Assimilation, however, brought closer identification with the mainstream. And as the Democratic Party moved to embrace the rights of minorities, there was a shift. Formerly stalwart Irish and Italian Democrats, dismayed and resentful of the focus on African-American grievances, shifted to the Republican

Becoming White

The Asian-white couples acknowledged that because their children are English monolingual and have little direct, sustained contact with the Asian parent's ethnic culture, they felt that their children would simply identify as white as they grow older. These patterns of identification are consistent with previous research that has demonstrated that English monolingualism and little exposure to the minority parent's culture increases the likelihood that Asian-white and Latino-white children will adopt a white identity rather than an Asian or Latino one.

The pattern of ethno-racial identification among the children of Latino-white couples is similar to that of children of Asian-white couples. For instance, a white woman married to a first-generation Mexican man explained, "I would always identify [my children] as white. I always considered them to be white. And to me, what does white mean? Caucasian is probably more specific." Others said that outsiders identify their children and the family as a whole as white, which shapes the way they see their children and themselves as a family unit. When a Latino-white couple was asked how outsiders react to them when they are together with their son, the second-generation Mexican husband said, "Just a regular American family." When we asked how people identify their son, he responded simply, "White, Caucasian," signaling that he was using the terms "American," "white," and "Caucasian" interchangeably.

Jennifer Lee and Frank D. Bean,
The Diversity Paradox: Immigration
and the Color Line in 21st Century America.
New York: Russell Sage Foundation, 2010. pp. 105–106.

Party. By the 1980s, the descendants of Irish and Italian immigrants—now "white" in the eyes of most Americans—were the defectors that delivered [Ronald] Reagan a victory in 1980 and a landslide in 1984.

Here's where things get muddy for those who believe in the destiny of demography. In the decades to come, a similar path might emerge for today's immigrants, and Latinos in particular, a product of the declining significance of racial differences. Interracial relationships are more common than they've ever been; in 2010, according to a report from the Pew Research Center, 15 percent of all new marriages were intermarriages. What's more, the large majority of these marriages occurred among whites, Latinos, and Asian Americans: 41 percent were between white and Latino partners, while 15 percent were between white and Asian partners.

It's hard to overstate the significance of this. Whites are the mainstream of American life, with tremendous representation in every area of our society. Through intermarriage, Latinos and Asian Americans are becoming similarly mainstreamed. Indeed, in politics, business, and culture, it's not hard to find examples of "minorities" who are indistinguishable from whites. For all intents and purposes, Texas senator Ted Cruz—the freshman lawmaker who helped drive the GOP into confrontation with President Obama—is understood as white, despite his heritage. More important, his children will *also* be understood as white.

While there are limits to the comparison between the Latinos and Asian Americans of today with their Irish and Italian predecessors—Latinos and Asian Americans span a wide range of nationalities—the basic point stands. These are two upwardly mobile groups that are rapidly assimilating with the white mainstream. If the pattern of the past holds, the future won't be majority-minority; it will be a white majority, where Spanish last names are common. And if that's the case, there's a chance that the GOP ends up getting a new crop of voters over the next two decades: Latinos and Asian Americans who have assimilated, become "white," and thus more conservative in their political preferences. As simply a function of time, the Republican Party will see a changing of the guard, and with it, a shift in its areas of focus. The civil libertarianism of Senator Rand Paul and the family-focused economic priorities of Utah senator Mike Lee provide a good idea of where the GOP might go in ten years.

The Future and the GOP

If the Republican Party can abandon its procedural radicalism—which, if recent polls are any indication, has taken a real toll on its brand—who is to say that this new mainstream won't find common cause with this future GOP? At the least, we can't say that the Republican Party is *clearly* doomed. A lot can change, and history suggests that the emerging Democratic majority is less likely than it looks.

But much depends on what the GOP does in the coming years. The Republican Party could alienate immigrants so much that Democratic identification becomes a matter of group interest. Like African Americans, Latino and Asian-American communities could come to understand conservative ideology—and not just the GOP—as a threat to their future advancement. In other words, perception of anti-immigrant animosity could linger for generations, as the descendants of assimilated Latinos and Asians continue to support Democrats out of group loyalty. In which case, the United States would become California writ large: a place where Latinos and Asians have turned decisively against the Republican Party, leaving it isolated from the levers of power—a rump faction in a more liberal America.

| *"No one wants to vote for a party that doesn't want you around."*

Boehner's Immigration Bill Halt Will Hurt GOP for Decades

Rachel Kleinfeld

Rachel Kleinfeld founded the Truman National Security Project and is a senior associate at the Carnegie Endowment for International Peace. In the following viewpoint, she argues that the Republican refusal to pass immigration reform will alienate Latino voters for a generation. She adds that the United States desperately needs to update its immigration policy to make it possible for employers to hire much-needed workers, both skilled and unskilled, who want to enter the country. She concludes that the current US immigration laws increase criminality by allowing the unscrupulous to exploit and prey on immigrants who want to enter the United States.

As you read, consider the following questions:

1. According to Kleinfeld, why is Boehner like Abraham Lincoln and Lyndon Johnson?

2. To whom do the majority of visas go, and why is this a problem, according to Kleinfeld?

3. What evidence does Kleinfeld provide to show that the hard right's emphasis on border security is a dodge?

House Speaker John Boehner might go down in history as the next Abraham Lincoln. Or at least Lyndon Johnson. But not in the way he might wish. Like those illustrious presidents, Boehner might have just made a decision that has scuttled his party's chances for decades to come.

Abraham Lincoln, a Republican, chose to emancipate the country's slaves, handing the former Confederacy to "Southern Democrats" for nearly a century. The tide didn't turn until Johnson, a Democrat, signed the Civil Rights Act knowing that he had just handed the South back to Republicans for a generation.

Boehner's decision to kill immigration reform will cost his party the Latino vote for at least that long. The fastest-growing demographic in the country, Latinos don't vote solely on immigration—in fact, given their strong religious and culturally conservative values, many pundits considered them potential swing voters. But no one wants to vote for a party that doesn't want you around.

The real loser is America's economy. California has a particular stake in changing the law because the face of immigration is changing. The majority of California's immigrants used to be poorer Latinos. Now the trend is toward college-educated Asians. Both are desperately needed by California's largest employers. But our immigration system, last significantly changed more than a quarter century ago, has become a patchwork of over-regulation and incoherent policies. We now give 75 percent of all visas to those with family members already here, leaving no room for economics. Uniting families is an important value, of course. But there are people who want to work hard, need jobs and don't have family in America—and a lot of people who want to hire them. Those forces will overwhelm the rule of law unless our laws align with our needs.

The world's best and brightest scientific minds aren't going to sneak into a country. They will go somewhere that values them.

Meanwhile, the agricultural industry still needs its seasonal workers, and they want to work here. As America learned the hard way during Prohibition, it's a bad idea to criminalize the forces of supply and demand. By ignoring these forces, our immigration policy—as Prohibition did—is pushing millions of otherwise law-abiding people into criminal activity and generating unintended side effects that hurt our laws, our communities and our economy.

Both parties had fringes that opposed change. The hard left claimed that immigration reform would bring down wages and cost "American" jobs. But the Democratic Senate overcame this opposition by passing a bill that enabled immigrant workers to get paid a decent wage and have benefits. Meanwhile, employers could no longer exploit immigrants here illegally and thereby keep wages down for American citizens. Everyone has to follow the law, so everyone gets a fairer shake.

The bigger myth, of course, is that there is a set number of jobs in the country for either "them" or "us." In reality, growing industries create more jobs: Just think of all those working in Internet industries that no one imagined 20 years ago.

The hard right claims we need more border security. This is a dodge. The reality is, nearly half of those here illegally came to the United States on legitimate visas and overstayed. The 9/11 [referring to the September 11, 2001, terrorist attacks on the United States] bombers came in through airports, and the failed Los Angeles Airport millennium bomber entered through Canada. More fences in the Southwest might feel more secure, but it's the bill's provisions to invest in people and technologies at all of our borders and visa-issuing agencies that make it strong on security.

Meanwhile, the modern Prohibition regime these fringes uphold does increase crime. Not from illegal immigrants themselves—most are law-abiding. But being here illegally creates a thriving market in human traffickers and other criminals who prey on immigrants and get away with it, knowing their victims are afraid to report crimes to American authorities.

California has wisely passed a series of new laws to try to address the spillover effects of our broken laws at the state level, including one that shields immigrants from deportation unless they've committed a violent crime. That should help the police in one state, but it's not enough.

As when he shut down the government, Boehner made another choice that harms America's economy for the sake of politics. Hard-hit Californians are doing their best to fix a leaky boat at the state level. They can't bail fast enough.

> *"A significant faction of conservatives see immigration reform as an existential threat to the country—and the Republican Party."*

Democrats May Benefit If the GOP Passes Immigration Reform

Sahil Kapur

Sahil Kapur is Talking Points Memo's senior congressional reporter and Supreme Court correspondent. In the following viewpoint, he reports that congressional Republicans fear that passing immigration reform will alienate core Republican voters, who then will not turn out in midterm elections. He adds that many Republicans are ideologically opposed to immigration reform in any case. Other Republicans feel that the party must change its stance if it wants to attract Hispanic voters in the long term, but those arguments seem to be drowned out in the worries about short-term losses.

As you read, consider the following questions:

1. According to Kapur, why do most Republican House members feel little need to represent Hispanic voters?

2. Who is John Sides, and why is he skeptical that immigration reform will depress turnout?

3. Who is Paul Ryan, and what does he say is the GOP attitude toward compromise on immigration reform?

Republicans may need immigration reform to avoid extinction in the long run, but there's a growing fear within the party that bringing it up now—as House GOP leaders have laid the groundwork to do by releasing a pro-reform blueprint—would depress conservative voter turnout and damage their standing in the 2014 elections.

Immigration and the Base

"No way it happens. I just don't see it going anywhere," said one House Republican aide, speaking candidly on condition of anonymity. "I think 2014 is a slam dunk to us otherwise and this would really piss off the base."

Dan Holler, a spokesman for Heritage Action [for America], the wealthy conservative lobbying group, warned GOP leaders not to follow through with reform. "The principles released by GOP leaders are a clear embrace of amnesty, and that could hurt the party in November," he told TPM [Talking Points Memo].

Some conservatives oppose reform on the merits and may be using these arguments to scare the party into inaction. But they may still have a point: midterm elections tend to be decided in large part by turnout, and a significant faction of conservatives see immigration reform as an existential threat to the country—and the Republican Party. Seeing their party abandon their views on such an emotionally charged issue could motivate them to stay home on Nov. 4.

"There is actually something to the premise," said Jack Pitney, a political scientist at Claremont McKenna College. "In the long run, Republicans have to do better with Hispanic voters. But candidates don't run in the long run—they run in

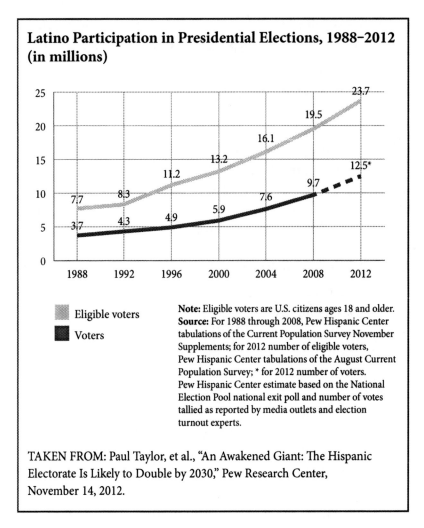

Latino Participation in Presidential Elections, 1988–2012 (in millions)

Eligible voters

Voters

Note: Eligible voters are U.S. citizens ages 18 and older.
Source: For 1988 through 2008, Pew Hispanic Center tabulations of the Current Population Survey November Supplements; for 2012 number of eligible voters, Pew Hispanic Center tabulations of the August Current Population Survey; * for 2012 number of voters. Pew Hispanic Center estimate based on the National Election Pool national exit poll and number of votes tallied as reported by media outlets and election turnout experts.

TAKEN FROM: Paul Taylor, et al., "An Awakened Giant: The Hispanic Electorate Is Likely to Double by 2030," Pew Research Center, November 14, 2012.

the election that's coming up. Most House Republicans do not have large Hispanic constituencies, and a decline in the base vote could cost them some otherwise winnable seats."

And as the *Cook Political Report* pointed out last year [2013], of the 108 minority-majority districts in the House, Republicans represent just nine of them. The average House Republican represents a district that is 75 percent white, which may mean these congressmen face little pressure from their constituents to take up the issue.

John Sides, a political science professor at George Washington University, doubts that reform would hurt Republicans much in the November congressional elections, arguing that few voters condition their turnout on "complete agreement" with their party's agenda. "For immigration reform to demobilize voters," he said, "I think it needs to be a focus of the campaign, and in the seats up for grabs, I'm not sure that would happen."

While veteran GOP operatives and nationally ambitious Republicans are content to accept some short-term political pain in order to secure the long-term gains of immigration reform, numerous influential conservatives are making their gripes known.

Movement Unlikely

The *Weekly Standard*'s Bill Kristol warned that an immigration debate "could blow up GOP chances for a good 2014." The *Washington Examiner*'s Philip Klein, deriding Speaker John Boehner as the "fool in the shower," argued that "in terms of the raw politics of 2014, introducing [immigration] now is bananas." He warned that passage of reform would "boost Democrats' prospects in 2014 by demoralizing the GOP base and elevating President Obama." The *National Review*'s Andrew McCarthy said the leadership's immigration plan was, among other things, "deeply offensive to the GOP's already disgruntled conservative base, ensuring that droves of them will sit out the 2014 midterms."

These are concerns that House Republican leaders will have to grapple with in the coming weeks and months as they weigh the merits of writing and advancing legislation that reflects their new blueprint, which endorses legal status (without the promise of citizenship) for people living in the country illegally.

House Budget [Committee] Chair Paul Ryan (WI), who supports reform, said it's "clearly in doubt" whether the House can pass an immigration bill that reaches the president's desk in 2014.

"This is not one of those issues where it has some kind of a deadline behind it, like, say, a government shutdown, which forces us into a compromise we might not like to take," Ryan said Sunday on ABC's *This Week*. He portrayed the GOP leadership's blueprint as a take-it-or-leave-it proposition—if even that: "This is a 'here are our standards, this is our approach, if you want to do it this way, this is what we're willing to do.' And we're still having a debate in our caucus about even that."

Many conservatives vigorously oppose immigration reform on substance, so the only reason GOP leaders are even considering it is the devastating longer-term politics on inaction. If that imperative is thrown in doubt, achieving reform this year will become a heavier lift, particularly ahead of the primaries, where numerous Republicans are fending off conservative challengers.

> "It's a reminder that our voting rights have always been under attack and probably always will be."

Voter ID Laws Could Disenfranchise 1 Million Young Minority Voters: Study

Trymaine Lee

Trymaine Lee is a senior reporter for the Huffington Post *and a former reporter for the* New York Times. *In the following viewpoint, he reports that numerous states have enacted voter identification (ID) laws and other restrictions on voting since the 2008 election. He says that these restrictions are likely to have a disproportionate effect on young minority voters, who are statistically less likely to have state IDs. He concludes that the laws seem to be part of a systematic effort by Republicans to depress minority turnout, and so hurt Democratic electoral chances.*

As you read, consider the following questions:

1. According to Lee, how many young minority voters could be unable to vote in November 2014?

2. By how much did the minority vote increase between 2004 and 2008 for different ethnic groups, according to Lee?

3. According to the viewpoint, where did the Department of Justice strike down voter ID laws, and on what grounds?

An estimated 700,000 young minority voters could be barred from voting in November [2014] because of photo ID laws passed across the country in recent years, according to a new study.

Turning Back the Clock

The number of minority voters under the age of 30 likely to be disenfranchised by these new voting laws—passed overwhelmingly by Republican-led legislatures across the country—is a conservative estimate, according to the study's authors. The actual number of voters in that category who could be disenfranchised is probably closer to 1 million, they said.

The projections include African Americans, Latinos, Asian Americans, Native Americans and Pacific Islanders.

"It's a reminder that our voting rights have always been under attack and probably always will be," said Cathy Cohen, a professor of political science at the University of Chicago who coauthored the report, "Turning Back the Clock on Voting Rights: The Impact of New Photo Identification Requirements on Young People of Color."

The study was created by the Black Youth Project, a nonpartisan, not-for-profit organization that aims to increase civic engagement and voter participation among minority youth.

"I don't think this is new, but I think the scale of it is new. . . . I think the brashness of hearing elected officials talk about how these laws will guarantee a win in their state for [Republican presidential nominee Mitt Romney]," Cohen told the *Huffington Post*. "And I think there is a willingness to be visible and vocal, which I think is new for us in the modern era."

The study estimates that the new laws, passed in 17 states, could cut turnout among young people of color in those states by between 538,000 and 696,000 voters, levels below turnout figures for those groups in the last two presidential elections.

Depressing Turnout

In 2004, 44 percent of blacks between 18 and 24 turned out to vote, the Associated Press [AP] reported. The Latino turnout for that year was 20.4 percent, and Asian Americans voted at a rate of 23.4 percent. In 2008, turnout among these groups exploded, with 52.3 percent of young blacks, 27.4 percent of young Latinos and 27.8 percent of young Asian Americans voting, according to the AP.

An overwhelming number of these voters cast ballots for President Barack Obama and Democrats.

Following the massive minority turnout in 2008, many states have passed stricter voting laws, which have included cutting early voting options and adding photo ID requirements. Minorities, including African Americans, Latinos and Asians, are less likely than their white counterparts to have a government-issued ID. Twenty-five percent of African Americans and 16 percent of Latinos lack such identification, compared to 9 percent of whites, according to the Brennan Center for Justice at New York University.

The new study offers insight into just how many voters could be turned away due to new restrictions on ID.

According to the report: Between 170,000 and 475,000 young black voters; 68,000 and 250,000 young Hispanic voters; 13,000 and 46,000 young Asian-American voters; 1,700 and 6,400 young Native American voters and 700 and 2,700 young Pacific Islander voters could be denied the right to vote or turned away at the polls for not having the proper credentials.

But Cohen said there is data that suggests that rates of valid ID ownership among people of color younger than 30 could be even lower than estimated. If younger minority voters have valid IDs at a rate of only 50 percent, she said, the impact of restrictive ID laws is more acute.

"We wanted to write a report that would really focus on young people of color, in part to draw a contrast between 2004 and 2008, where we saw a really dramatic increase of young people of color going to the polls, expanding the democracy," Cohen said. "Now we face a situation where in fact maybe 700,000 or more young people could be immobilized."

The study's authors estimate that the drop in turnout among these groups could not only have an impact on those able to cast a ballot in the presidential election, but could also affect a number of hotly contested House races.

Key States

The depleted turnout could likely play a major role in battleground states such as Florida and Pennsylvania, both of which have enacted new voting laws.

In Florida, more than 100,000 young people of color could be demobilized, according to the report. In Pennsylvania, where the state Supreme Court recently upheld the state's photo ID law, an estimated 37,000 to 44,000 minority voters could be affected, the report found.

What's at play, said Jon Rogowski, a professor at Washington University in St. Louis and a coauthor of the report, is a confluence of factors which includes not just the passing of new laws, which he believes Republicans have passed to target likely Democratic voters, but also a waning of energy from the historic 2008 election of President Obama.

Minority Turnout in 2012

Without any primary challengers, Barack Obama's campaign only needed to prepare for the general election. And prepare it did. The vaunted turnout machine that produced near record voter participation in 2008 got the job done again in 2012. Although absolute levels of turnout were down, Obama succeeded in turning out people from the demographic groups that the campaign targeted. Generally, campaigns find it hard to get young people and racial and ethnic minorities to the polls on Election Day, but these groups made up a larger than usual slice of the electorate in 2012. Young people (those aged 18–29) increased their share of the electorate to 19 percent, its highest percentage since exit poll data have been gathered. In addition, nonwhites made up fully 28 percent of the total electorate, an increase of 2 percentage points over 2008. That the Obama campaign boosted minority turnout even with a sluggish economy that was particularly unforgiving to racial and ethnic minorities is a testament to its get-out-the-vote campaign's success.

Also indicative of the Obama campaign's relative strength, it achieved a near sweep of the battleground states, winning nine of the ten states that both campaigns targeted. . . . In the end, Obama retained all the states that he won in 2008 except Indiana, which had been a fluke victory the last time around, and North Carolina, which he won in 2008 by a mere 14,000 votes.

Marc J. Hetherington,
"The Election: How the Campaign Mattered,"
in Michael Nelson, ed. The Elections of 2012.
Thousand Oaks, CA: SAGE, 2014.

"I think that the first thing that stands out in the aftermath of 2008 is that the population for which we heard the most about being energized for the first time in large numbers, that came out for President Obama, are exactly the kind of voters to be most immobilized by the new voter ID requirements," Rogowski said. "Not only are we likely to see lower numbers of people of color turning out to vote, but the political potency of those groups will also be reduced."

According to Cohen and Rogowski, more than two-thirds of U.S. states have sought to make voting harder by layering restrictions on the process in which voters cast a ballot. Nine states require voters to show government-issued ID to vote, while eight others have enacted similar requirements while offering limited alternatives.

Only two of these laws were enacted before the 2008 election.

"While we are disheartened to see the apparently systematic way in which the minority youth vote is being undermined, we are committed to meeting this assault with redoubled efforts to ensure that everyone who is eligible to vote can and does vote," Marc H. Morial, president and CEO [chief executive officer] of the National Urban League, said in a statement. "Nothing less than the future of our political process is at stake."

The Department of Justice [DOJ] has struck down voter ID laws in Texas, Florida, South Carolina and Wisconsin this year [2012] under the Voting Rights Act, which mandates that states with a history of racially discriminatory voting procedures get their laws cleared by the DOJ.

Some have maintained that the new laws are meant to protect the democratic process, not erode it, by making voter fraud more difficult. But Democratic leaders, civil rights groups and voting rights organizations and activists have said that the new laws are clearly an assault on minority voters, the elderly and the poor, many of whom face social and economic hurdles that make acquiring the required documents more difficult. Others, including Attorney Gen. Eric Holder, have likened the laws to Jim Crow–era poll taxes and other nefarious policies designed to keep African Americans from voting.

"Along the way, we have heard certain state lawmakers allude to the likely electoral impact of these kinds of laws," Rogowski said. "It's difficult to try to imagine what other, or in what other kinds of ways, they expect these laws to have electoral impacts."

"I think it's a concerted effort to disenfranchise Democratic voters, and those voters that most often won't have these types of ID," Cohen said. "I don't want to get into the hearts and minds of the Republican legislatures that they meant to disenfranchise black people, but they probably meant to disenfranchise Democratic voters and the more vulnerable Democratic voters."

> *"We don't have very good data to support the claim that voter ID laws will disproportionately disenfranchise progressive women. In fact . . . these laws may hurt conservative women instead."*

Ladies' Choice: Voter ID Laws Might Suppress the Votes of Women. Republican Women.

Dahlia Lithwick

Dahlia Lithwick is a contributing editor at Newsweek *and a senior editor at* Slate. *In the following viewpoint, she argues that the effect of voter identification (ID) laws on turnout is uncertain. She contends that Republicans have passed such laws to drive down minority turnout, but that the laws may also have an effect on married or divorced women who change their names and whose IDs may therefore not match the names on voter rolls. Lithwick says that Republican women are more likely to marry and divorce, as well as to change their names when they marry; therefore, ID laws may actually reduce turnout among Republican female voters.*

As you read, consider the following questions:

1. What evidence does Lithwick provide that women have helped Democrats in recent elections?

2. What does Lithwick say is wrong with the Brennan Center for Justice study, which is used to say that ID laws will disenfranchise women?

3. According to Sam Issacharoff, why might voter ID laws not have much effect on minority turnout?

Last June [2013] the U.S. Supreme Court struck down a key part of the Voting Rights Act, resulting in several states, among them Texas and North Carolina, racing to enact draconian new voter ID laws. While the first wave of attention focused on the ways such laws disproportionately impact minority voters, young voters, and the elderly, a slew of articles this past weekend [in October 2013] point out that voter ID laws may also significantly suppress women's votes. Indeed some have even suggested that this is the next front in the war on women, and suppressing female votes is part of the GOP's concerted effort to ensure victories in states like Texas, where women like Wendy Davis threaten to topple the GOP with the support of female voters. It's beyond disputing that women have ensured that Democrats, up to and including President [Barack] Obama, have achieved major wins in recent elections. Female voters decided 22 of 23 Senate races in the 2012 election.

Which Women Will Be Affected?

But a closer look at whether voter ID laws will invariably harm liberal women and Democratic candidates at the polls suggests that something more interesting, and more complicated, may be going on here. We don't actually have very good data to support the claim that voter ID laws will disproportionately disenfranchise progressive women. In fact some election law experts tell me the opposite may be true: These laws may hurt conservative women instead.

The problem around women and voter ID is neither new nor complicated: Women often change their names when they marry and divorce. Men don't. Because some of the new voter ID bills frequently demand that a voter's name correspond to her most up-to-date, legally recognized name at the polls, they erect a barrier for women who haven't kept their ID current to reflect changing marital status. And since, at least according to one source, American women change their names about 90 percent of the time when they marry or divorce, they are at significantly higher risk of being unable to provide an ID that matches their current legal name.

As the many articles considering the problem suggest, in some states that is about to get even worse. As *ThinkProgress* reported last week, the new Texas voter ID law demands that "constituents show original documents verifying legal proof of a name change, whether it is a marriage license, divorce decree, or court ordered change." Photocopies will not be accepted. If you don't have those original documents, you must pay a minimum of $20 for new copies. So in some states, female voters face two hurdles—showing they are who they claim to be and producing original documents indicating that they really are married and divorced.

Uncertain Data

Interestingly, almost everyone arguing that progressive women will be disproportionately harmed by these laws cites a single study done in 2006 by the Brennan Center for Justice. According to that study, only "48% of voting-age women with ready access to their U.S. birth certificates have a birth certificate with current legal name—and only 66% of voting-age women with ready access to *any* proof of citizenship have a document with current legal name." The survey concluded that "using 2000 census citizen voting-age population data, this means that as many as **32 million** voting-age women may have available only proof of citizenship documents that do not reflect their current name." (Emphasis theirs.)

But the Brennan study looked only at proof of citizenship documents, not photo IDs, so it may not in fact prove the argument being advanced here. The Brennan study made no findings with respect to a gender differential on current photo IDs. I asked around, but I was unable to find many good studies that showed whether women would be disproportionately disenfranchised by Texas-style voter ID laws. That doesn't mean that photo ID laws won't disproportionately affect women. But it does mean the Brennan study doesn't quite prove it.

Ineffective Disenfranchisement

Moreover, when I spoke to several election law experts about the problem, more than one of them confirmed my suspicion that women who change their names may tend to skew more conservative than women who don't. Or as Sam Issacharoff, a professor at NYU [New York University] law school, explained it to me, "During the 2012 presidential election, I thought the Pennsylvania [voter ID] law was unlikely to have any partisan effect because the way the ID law was drafted there was likely to have an impact on more Republican than Democratic voters, in part for the reasons you identify. Women in particular who are married and change their name I thought were likely not Democratic voters."

Something else to consider: If the slew of new voter ID laws may hit divorced women hardest, consider that women in red states in fact have much higher divorce and remarriage rates. And women in the South have especially high remarriage rates. So it's not at all clear that liberal women will be disenfranchised in greater numbers than their conservative counterparts. I'm told that women generally get hassled more at the polls because they rarely resemble the image on their photo ID in the first place.

The truth is that if Republicans want to scuttle Wendy Davis' electoral chances [for governor of Texas], there are demonstrably easier ways of getting the job done. After all, the same Texas legislature that passed the restrictive voter ID law was found by a federal court to have intentionally tried to pass a redistricting plan that would have redistricted Wendy Davis out of business. And, overall, there is good data to suggest that voter ID laws will clearly disenfranchise Hispanic and African American voters, poor voters, students, and other groups that skew Democratic. But the issue of women and voter ID is less clear-cut.

Ultimately, the data is still fairly bad on both sides of the voter ID debate, although it's pretty much delusional on the vote fraud side. NYU's Issacharoff sums it up this way: "Republicans think as a matter of deep faith that there is a lot of in-person, Election Day voter fraud. Many Democrats believe that the ID laws and the like have resulted in a lot of voter suppression. But there is precious little empirical evidence of either. The in-person vote fraud stuff is nonsense. But the ID laws seem to target populations that are isolated from mainstream society and do not participate. Mean, offensive, hopefully unconstitutional, and all that. Just not all that effective, best I can tell."

All this ambiguity in the data is why Judge Richard Posner stirred up such a hornet's nest last week when he admitted to *HuffPost Live*'s Mike Sacks that he made a mistake when he wrote the decision in 2007 upholding Indiana's voter ID law. He now believes the dissenters in the voter ID case had it right. But beyond questions about whether judges should recant their own decisions in the media, Posner's mea culpa forces all of us to contend with our assumptions about the motivations behind voter ID laws and the proof we have to support them. And when it comes to female voters, it may be that what looks like everyday Republican voter ID deviousness will prove to be the sound of them shooting themselves in the foot.

> *"Even if Democratic congressional can-*
> *didates won the popular vote by seven*
> *percentage points nationwide, they still*
> *would not have gained control of the*
> *House."*

In the House, a Deck Stacked for Republicans

Dana Milbank

Dana Milbank is a columnist for the Washington Post. *In the following viewpoint, he reports on figures from the 2012 elections showing that there were more Democratic votes cast for House seats even though Republicans won the chamber. He says that this is in part because Democratic voters are concentrated in particular urban districts. Mostly, though, he blames Republican gerrymandering, or the careful drawing of district lines to give political parties an electoral advantage. Because of gerrymandering, he says, in future elections Democrats need to win the popular vote by at least nine points to gain a House majority. That is possible but unlikely, which means that Republicans are likely to continue to hold control of the House.*

As you read, consider the following questions:

1. Why do Republicans say they have as much of a mandate as President Obama, and why does Milbank not agree with them?

2. What does Milbank say is an ominous development for Democrats?

3. According to Milbank, do Republicans have a permanent House majority?

As a new Congress convenes, it has become an unquestioned truth among Republicans that their party has as much of a mandate as President [Barack] Obama because voters returned them to power in the House.

Democratic Disadvantage

The mantra has been intoned by John Boehner, Paul Ryan, Mitch McConnell, Newt Gingrich, Grover Norquist and many other party eminences, and there is a certain logic to saying that the voters, by giving Republicans the House, were asking for divided government.

But the claim to represent the voters' will doesn't add up.

The final results from the November [2012] election were completed Friday, and they show that Democratic candidates for the House outpolled Republicans nationwide by nearly 1.4 million votes and more than a full percentage point—a greater margin than the preliminary figures showed in November. And that's just the beginning of it: A new analysis finds that even if Democratic congressional candidates won the popular vote by seven percentage points nationwide, they still would not have gained control of the House.

The analysis, by Ian Millhiser at the liberal Center for American Progress using data compiled by the nonpartisan *Cook Political Report*, finds that even if Democrats were to win the popular vote by a whopping nine percentage points—a political advantage that can't possibly be maintained year after year—they would have a tenuous eight-seat majority.

In a very real sense, the Republican House majority is impervious to the will of the electorate. Thanks in part to deft redistricting based on the 2010 census, House Republicans may be protected from the vicissitudes of the voters for the next decade. For Obama and the Democrats, this is an ominous development: The House Republican majority is durable, and it isn't necessarily sensitive to political pressure and public opinion.

According to the Jan. 4 final tally by *Cook*'s David Wasserman after all states certified their votes, Democratic House candidates won 59,645,387 votes in November to the Republicans' 58,283,036, a difference of 1,362,351. On a percentage basis, Democrats won, 49.15 percent to 48.03 percent.

A Built-in Advantage

This in itself is an extraordinary result: Only three or four other times in the past century has a party lost the popular vote but won control of the House. But computer-aided gerrymandering is helping to make such undemocratic results the norm—to the decided advantage of Republicans, who controlled state governments in 21 states after the 2010 census, almost double the 11 for Democrats.

To be sure, Democrats tend to be just as flagrant as Republicans when they have the chance to gerrymander. And the Republican advantage isn't entirely because of redistricting; Democrats have lopsided majorities in urban clusters, so the overall popular vote overstates their competitiveness in other districts. An analysis by FairVote found that nonpartisan redistricting would only partially close the gap, which comes also from the disappearance of ticket-splitting voters who elected centrist Democrats.

But the 2012 House results show the redrawing of districts to optimize Republican representation clearly had an impact.

Popular Vote vs. House Seats in Key States with Republican Gerrymandering

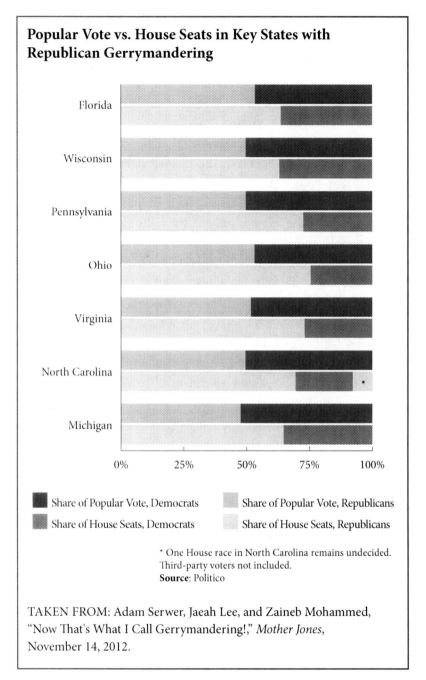

* One House race in North Carolina remains undecided.
Third-party voters not included.
Source: Politico

TAKEN FROM: Adam Serwer, Jaeah Lee, and Zaineb Mohammed, "Now That's What I Call Gerrymandering!," *Mother Jones*, November 14, 2012.

Consider three states won by Obama in 2012 where Republicans dominated the redistricting: In Pennsylvania, Democrats won just five of 18 House seats; in Virginia, Democrats won three of 11; and in Ohio, Democrats won four of 16.

Using Wasserman's tally, Millhiser ranked districts by the Republican margin of victory and calculated that for Democrats to have won the 218 seats needed for a House majority they would have had to have added 6.13 percentage points to their popular-vote victory margin of 1.12 points.

To put the Republican advantage in perspective, Democrats could win the House only if they do significantly better than Republicans did in their landslide year of 2010 (when they had a 6.6-point advantage). That's not impossible—Democrats did it in 2006 and 2008—but it's difficult. Republicans don't have a permanent House majority, but they will go into the next several elections with an automatic head start. For many, the biggest political threat comes not from Democrats but from conservative primary challengers.

In theory, the Supreme Court could decide before then that this rigged system denies Americans fair and effective representation. But this won't happen anytime soon. For now, Democrats need to recognize that the Republican House majority will respond only sluggishly to the usual levers of democracy.

> "While gerrymandering contributes a
> bit to this [partisan] bias, its impact is
> marginal—the big culprit is single-seat,
> winner-take-all districts themselves,
> combined with the overconcentration of
> Democratic voters."

How the Voting Rights Act Hurts Democrats and Minorities

Steven Hill

Steven Hill is the author of 10 Steps to Repair American Democracy: A More Perfect Union: 2012 Election Edition *and* Europe's Promise: Why the European Way Is the Best Hope in an Insecure Age. *In the following viewpoint, he argues that the Republican advantage in the House is the result of the Voting Rights Act (VRA) and of Democratic Party efforts that have created districts packed with minority voters. These districts elect minority representatives. However, they also seal minority, usually Democratic, voters off from other districts, which ends up reducing the number of districts Democrats can win. Hill con-*

Steven Hill, "How the Voting Rights Act Hurts Democrats and Minorities," *Atlantic*, June 17, 2013 © 2013 The Atlantic Media Co., as first published in The Atlantic Magazine. All rights reserved. Distributed by Tribune Content Agency, LLC. Reproduced by permission.

cludes that majority-minority districts have given Republicans a built-in advantage. He suggests a system of proportional representation, rather than winner take all, to create a fairer electoral playing field.

As you read, consider the following questions:

1. According to Hill, what evidence shows that Section 5 of the Voting Rights Act is still needed?

2. What race-based remedy for historical discrimination does the GOP promote and why, according to Hill?

3. What does Hill say would be the most mutually beneficial way to restructure voting for Democrats and minorities?

Civil rights are on the nation's docket in a major way. Sometime this month, the U.S. Supreme Court will decide an important voting rights case, *Shelby County v. Holder*, in addition to another case involving racial discrimination in higher education and two potentially landmark cases on gay marriage. By the end of June, the nation's civil rights profile may look quite different.

In *Shelby County*, the justices are weighing whether the 1965 Voting Rights Act should continue to apply specially to designated regions of the country with ugly histories of racial discrimination. These regions, including the entire state of Alabama as well as eight other states and more than 60 counties, currently must seek "preclearance" from the Department of Justice for any changes to their voting laws and practices (changes can still be challenged after enactment). Officials in Shelby County, Alabama, say "times have changed," that Shelby County is no longer the cesspool of Jim Crow racism it once was, and so the high court should overturn the preclearance requirement, known in legal parlance as Section 5.

Despite the protestations of Shelby County and other jurisdictions, mountains of evidence show that there is little doubt that Section 5 is still needed, including in Shelby County. If anything, preclearance requirements should probably be extended to more parts of the country. Every election reveals new and deviously crafted efforts at voter suppression, from voter ID laws to intimidation and long lines at the polls that by coincidence seem to afflict minority precincts more than others. Republican legislators in various states continue to push laws that will clearly have a disproportionate impact on minority voters. Section 5's preclearance has been a powerful disincentive against discrimination in elections that, sadly, is still very present today. If the Supreme Court guts Section 5—as voting rights advocates fear will happen, given the court's conservative majority—the nation will be jumping off a cliff into unknown territory.

But it would be a mistake to think that, though many Republicans want to see Section 5 struck down, they oppose other sections of the Voting Rights Act. Quite the contrary: The GOP has found the VRA to be a great ally. It turns out the act, as traditionally applied, has helped the party win a great number of legislative races. It also has become a potent obstacle to the Democrats retaking the U.S. House of Representatives.

Beginning in the civil rights era in the 1960s, the Republican Party—the party of Lincoln—became the loudest opponent of race-based remedies to discrimination, whether in school admissions, hiring, or minority representation. The Democrats, once the party of segregation (some people forget that segregationists George Wallace and Strom Thurmond were elected governors of Alabama and South Carolina, respectively, as Democrats) did a dramatic about-face in the 1960s and became the party of civil rights. Acting under the legal strength and moral authority of the Voting Rights Act, the Democrats led the charge to draw so-called "majority-minority districts"—ones packed so full of minority voters that they usually resulted in electing a minority representative, as intended. The number of minority representatives jumped exponentially from the 1960s through the 1980s, with the number of black House members increasing from five to 24 by 1989.

But just in time for the redistricting in 1990, some enterprising Republicans began noticing a rather curious fact: The drawing of majority-minority districts not only elected more minorities, it also had the effect of bleeding minority voters out of all the surrounding districts. Given that minority voters were the most reliably Democratic voters, that made all of the neighboring districts more Republican. The black, Latino, and Asian representatives mostly were replacing white Democrats, and the increase in minority representation was coming at the expense of electing fewer Democrats. The Democrats had been tripped up by a classic catch-22, as had minority voters: Even as legislatures were becoming more diverse, they were ironically becoming less friendly to the agenda of racial minorities.

Newt Gingrich embraced this strategy of drawing majority-minority districts for GOP advantage, as did the Bush administration Justice Department prior to the 1991 redistricting, even as GOP activists like now chief justice John Roberts campaigned against the VRA because they opposed any race-based remedies. The tipping point was the 1994 midterm elections, when the GOP captured the U.S. House of Representatives for the first time in 35 years and Gingrich became speaker. Many experts on both the left and the right, from the *Nation*'s Ari Berman and prominent GOP election lawyer Ben Ginsberg (who spearheaded the 1991 effort to maximize the number of majority-minority districts), attribute the Republican success that year to the drawing of majority-minority districts; indeed, African-American membership in the House reached its highest level ever, at 40.

VRA districts undoubtedly played a role in the GOP takeover, but they were not the only factor, since Republicans made big gains that year in lots of places outside the South. But in the hardscrabble battles of the 50-50 nation, any advantage at all was embraced, and prominent Republicans like Ginsberg and Gingrich became the loudest proponents of drawing majority-minority districts. Many Republicans still promote this strategy today, and it's the only race-based remedy the GOP has supported in the modern era. The party has been more than willing to shelve its ideology when it suited their naked political interests.

So in *Shelby County*, many Republicans are trying to have their cake and eat it too. They want the Supreme Court to gut Section 5 of the Voting Rights Act, which prevents them from enacting various voter-suppression laws. But they want to preserve the other parts of the VRA that provide the legal impetus for drawing majority-minority districts. One can't help but admire their cleverness.

Meanwhile, it's only going to get worse for the Democrats. Not only has the drawing of majority-minority districts led to fewer elected Democrats, but today single-seat districts themselves have become a huge barrier to Democrats retaking the House. That's because shifting partisan demographics have left Democratic voters more geographically concentrated than Republican voters. The problem is easy to see in urban areas, where Democratic votes are heavily concentrated. Urban Democrat House members—a large number of whom are minority—win with huge majorities, but winning a district with 80 percent doesn't help the party gain any more seats than winning with 60 percent. It just bleeds more Democratic voters out of the surrounding districts.

Yet it's not just urban districts that reflect the tilted partisan landscape. Election simulations have shown that partisan demographics—even more than the gerrymandering of district lines—give the GOP a natural, built-in edge in a majority of House districts. Those simulations predict that in 2014 the GOP will maintain control of the House even if Democrats

Keeping the Vote from Blacks

By 1877 southern white Democrats had overthrown every new state government and established state constitutions that stripped black citizens of their political rights. To circumvent the Fourteenth and Fifteenth Amendments, legislators created clever devices that would disenfranchise black citizens for the next eighty years. These included not only literacy and "understanding" tests, poll taxes, and residency and property requirements; among these devices was also a "grandfather clause" that exempted white men and their male descendants from literacy tests and property qualifications if they had voted prior to January 1, 1867. That date was important because it was three years before the Fifteenth Amendment guaranteed black citizens that right and just before the all-white Democratic Party primary barred black candidates from political participation. . . . The intent of the laws was explicit: "The plan," said one Mississippi official in 1890, "is to invest permanently the powers of government in the hands of the people who ought to have them—the white people."

The laws were disastrous for newly empowered black citizens. In Louisiana 130,000 had been registered to vote in 1896. By 1904 only 1,342 remained to exercise the franchise, if whites permitted it. Virginia's 147,000 black voters were reduced to 21,000. Eighty-three percent of Alabama's electorate was again white in 1906, compared to only 2 percent of theoretically eligible black adults. . . . By the early twentieth century black disenfranchisement, like economic and social segregation, was complete throughout the South, and it remained almost unchanged for the next sixty years.

Gary May, Bending Toward Justice:
The Voting Rights Act and the Transformation of American
Democracy. *New York: Basic Books, 2013.*

win the nationwide House vote by nearly 10 percentage points. This dynamic was illustrated in the 2012 election, when President Obama defeated Mitt Romney by nearly five million votes nationwide, but Romney's vote was more efficiently dispersed—he won 226 House districts to Obama's 209. That means Democrats can win a House majority only if their candidates win numerous districts won by Romney, a steep uphill climb. This explains the oddity of 2012, when the Democrats won the most votes nationwide in House races but still ended up with a minority of seats.

Many analysts incorrectly blame this partisan tilt on the extreme gerrymandering of legislative districts for partisan advantage. While gerrymandering contributes a bit to this bias, its impact is marginal—the big culprit is single-seat, winner-take-all districts themselves, combined with the overconcentration of Democratic voters. These partisan demographics have made it far easier for GOP map drawers in Georgia, Ohio, Pennsylvania, and elsewhere not only to pack Democratic voters into fewer districts but also to pick off many white Democratic House members and "racialize" the Democratic Party. In 1991, white Democrats held 81 of 133 House seats in the South, but today that number has dwindled to 18 out of 145. This is why some zealous GOP activists have mounted a campaign to award presidential electors by congressional districts instead of on a statewide basis. Doing so would have resulted in Romney winning the presidency, even though he lost the national popular vote by a sizable margin.

This Republican edge also exists in most state legislatures, and it has been consistent for decades. But it was masked by the previous success of southern Democrats in conservative districts, which was a legacy of Jim Crow and of Democrats being the party of segregation. Today, it's like having a footrace in which one side (the Republicans) starts out 10 yards ahead of the other (the Democrats).

Democratic leaders have tried to address this asymmetrical battlefield by controlling redistricting wherever and whenever they can, but they've had decreasing success as these partisan demographics have become more deeply rooted into the political landscape. Unfortunately for the Democrats, this fundamental dilemma over majority-minority districts strikes at the heart of its identity as a political party. It's to the party's credit that it walked away from its segregationist past and became the party of civil rights, but in 2013 the reality is that majority-minority districts and the continued use of one-seat, winner-take-all districts have painted the Democrats into a corner.

The most mutually beneficial arrangement for the Democrats and racial minorities would be for the electoral system to evolve from the current single-seat blueprint to a multi-seat system elected by proportional representation. With proportional voting, parties win seats in proportion to their vote share—in a five-seat district, a party winning 40 percent of the vote wins two seats instead of nothing, and a party with 60 percent of the vote wins three seats instead of everything.

That would allow minorities to win their fair share of representation without gerrymandering any districts, and to do so without hurting the electoral chances of other Democratic Party candidates. In the South, such a plan would elect more black *and* white Democrats; it also would enfranchise more minority voters, since in every southern state a majority of the state's black voters continue to live in white majority districts where they have little to no influence. A proportional system would make these voters influential no matter where they live.

Interestingly, the U.S. has not always used single-seat districts to elect House members. In 1967 the Democrats controlling Congress passed a law that mandated the use of single-seat districts for federal House races, both to prevent some recalcitrant southern Democrats from going to statewide winner-take-all elections to dilute the black vote and also as a way to facilitate the gerrymandering of majority-minority districts. Ironically, now it's that very same district-based system that is dragging the Democrats underwater. Passing a proportional representation method looks unlikely in the short term, but it can be done by mere statute without a constitutional change. Rep. Mel Watt, a North Carolina Democrat, introduced legislation to allow states this option not that long ago. Democrats could partially outfox the GOP by embracing Watt's approach and pushing for a "home-rule" option within the 50 states for the use of proportional systems in U.S. House races as a voting rights remedy.

In the meantime, the GOP must be cackling with glee at the Democrats' dilemmas, even as Republicans champion more majority-minority districts while fighting against every other race-based remedy to historical discrimination. Politics is often like a game of chess—a very down and dirty version—and one can't help but conclude that the Republicans are outsmarting the Democrats in this gambit.

> *"There are plenty of reasons the Demo-crats won't win back the House. But it's not impossible that they will."*

The Democrats Can Still Win the House

Harry J. Enten

Harry J. Enten has written about politics and statistics at the blog Margin of Error *and the* Guardian. *In the following view-point, he argues that a Democratic victory in the House is not likely, but, despite the arguments of many, it is not impossible. Claims that Democrats need a seven point lead in the popular vote to win the House are overstated, he argues, and predictions based on early polling are in any case too far from Election Day to be certain. He concludes that Democrats face an uphill battle for the House, but that Republican victory is not assured.*

As you read, consider the following questions:

1. According to Enten, why is a uniform swing of votes an inexact measure of actual election outcomes?

2. What evidence does Enten provide to show that early estimates of competitive seats are often inaccurate?

3. Does Enten believe that national House ballots are biased against Democrats? Why, or why not?

I don't believe the Democrats will win back the House of Representatives in 2014. President [Barack] Obama's low approval rating, combined with the usual midterm loss and normal movement away from the White House party on the national House ballot, should keep Republicans in control. Yet, there's a difference between thinking whether the Democrats "will" win back the House or whether they "can" win it back.

Democratic Lead May Be Enough

Right now, the Democrats hold a lead of about 4–5pt per the HuffPollster and RealClearPolitics average. Many have concluded that this lead would not be enough to take back the House, if the election were held today. However, I believe that it quite likely *would be enough*.

How so? Let's address a bunch of reasons people expect that a 4–5pt Democratic lead on the national House ballot would result in Republicans still holding the House—and then show why I think those could be wrong.

1. A uniform shift of 4–5pt on all House seats would still leave Republicans winning a majority of seats.

North Carolina Republican congressman Robert Pittenger was the "median" representative in 2012. Half the races were decided by more than his 6.1pt margin and half were decided by less. Given that Democrats won the national House vote by 1.4pt, a uniform swing across all districts would imply that Democrats would need to win the national House vote by 7.5pt to take back the House.

Count me as one of the people who does not believe in uniform swings. It's not that the uniform swing is uninformative; it's that it is very inexact. There are many factors that go into House races, including challenger quality, money spent, and whether or not the incumbent is running for re-election. Most of those are unknown at this point for key races.

You only need to look at the 2006 election to get an idea. Back in 2004, Republicans won the national House vote by 2.6pt. They won the median district by a little over 10pt. In other words, there was that same 7.5pt pro-Republican bias between the national House vote and the median district in 2004 as there was last year.

When we examine 2006, we see the bias simply didn't hold. Democrats only won the national House vote by 8pt, which should have given them the thinnest of majorities per a uniform swing. Instead, they took 233, or 13 more, seats than a uniform swing implied.

The 218th seat won by the Democrats belonged to Leonard Boswell, who had actually taken the seat easily in 2004. He had health problems, which led to a closer than expected re-election campaign. Boswell, with a winning margin of 5.4pt, might have survived even if the national Democratic margin had been closer to 3pt.

My own math, taking into account redistricting in 2011, says a 3pt Democratic win in the national vote and a takeover of the House would not be nearly as likely as in 2006; but a 4 or 5pt victory would probably do the trick.

Too Early to Know

2. The experts say there are very few seats up for grabs.

The indispensable *Cook Political Report* has only had 13 Democratic-held seats listed in the relatively competitive toss-up or "lean" category. Of course, Democrats need to take 17 seats to win the House. The ratings reflect, among other things, a lack of strong challengers for the Democrats and lack of retirements by Republicans.

The thing is that expert ratings (like most polling) are not all that predictive a year out from an election. At this point in the 2006 cycle, there were 17 Republican seats in the lean or toss-up categories. That's well short of the 30 seats that Democrats would ultimately take from Republicans. At this point in the 2010 cycle, there were 28 Democratic seats in the lean or toss-up category. Republicans, of course, went on to gain *63 seats* in 2010.

It's not until later in the cycle when individual seat rankings become quite useful. That's when potential challengers and incumbents read the national environment and decide to run or not. Chances are that if the 4–5pt Democratic lead holds, the individual seat rankings will reflect that edge. For now, individual seat rankings probably aren't all that helpful to understanding which way and how hard the wind is blowing.

3. The Abramowitz model says Democrats need something like a 13pt margin on the national House ballot.

Alan Abramowitz's national House ballot to seats model seems to have unusual sway among some. The model is elegant in the sense that it does a good job of trying to map the midterm penalty and how much exposure the majority party has, in a minimalistic fashion. The problem is that some don't seem to quite understand how the model should work.

It's not a straight national vote-to-seat equation. It's built for early September of a midterm year. Abramowitz isn't saying that a 13pt Democratic margin in the national House ballot on Election Day is what Democrats need to take over the House. What he is saying is that a 13pt lead in September is likely to shrink because of the natural movement away from the White House party on the national House ballot during the course of the election year.

Moreover, the model is inexact. It would be within the margin of error of the model for Democrats to take back the House with a 2pt September lead on the national House ballot. In 2010, the model forecasted a Republican gain of 45 seats per my calculation. That was 18 seats off the final Republican gain of 63 seats.

Abramowitz's forecast is a good starting point for understanding how uphill is the Democrats' task in taking back the House, but it is far from perfect.

Not Impossible

4. The final national House ballot surveys are biased against Republicans.

Charlie Cook has a rule that you subtract 2pt from the Democratic margin on the final national House ballot to know how the national House vote is actually going to pan out. That may have worked over five years ago, though it doesn't seem to work anymore. In 2008, 2010, and 2012, the Real-ClearPolitics average of the national House ballot underestimated the actual Democratic standing in the national House vote. So, there's no reason to think the final national House ballot will overstate the Democrats' standing in 2014.

There are plenty of reasons the Democrats won't win back the House. But it's not impossible that they will. If the same national environment that is producing a 4–5pt lead on the national House ballot still exists in a year's time, Democrats may very well win back the House.

Periodical and Internet Sources Bibliography

The following articles have been selected to supplement the diverse views presented in this chapter.

Jonathan Chait — "Which Party Benefits from Immigration Reform?," *New York*, June 18, 2013.

Elise Foley — "House Democrats Aim to Push Past GOP on Immigration," *Huffington Post*, March 25, 2014.

Jaime Fuller — "Why Voting Rights Is the Democrats' Most Important Project in 2014," *Washington Post*, April 10, 2014.

Alex Isenstadt — "Democrats: Cede the House to Save the Senate," Politico, January 29, 2014.

Andrew Kohut — "The Demographics Behind the Democrats' 2014 Troubles," *Wall Street Journal*, March 30, 2014.

Leslie Marshall — "Why Democrats Will Win the House in 2014," *U.S. News & World Report*, March 13, 2013.

Stephen Ohlemacher — "The GOP Advantage: Geography or Gerrymandering?," ABC News, March 31, 2014.

Ed O'Keefe — "House Democrats Plot Strategy Against Long Odds to Win Back Chamber," *Washington Post*, February 12, 2014.

Rick Perlstein — "Why a Democratic Majority Is Not Demographic Inevitability (Part Two: The Politics of Immigration Reform)," *Nation*, March 20, 2013.

Greg Sargent — "The Democrats' Latest Long-Shot Strategy on Immigration," *Washington Post*, March 25, 2014.

OPPOSING
VIEWPOINTS®
SERIES

CHAPTER 2

How Does the Democratic Party Relate to Important Voting Groups?

Chapter Preface

The millennial generation refers to people born from the early 1980s to the early 2000s. Millennial voters have been much more likely to vote Democratic than their older peers in elections since 2004, according to a November 3, 2011, article at the Pew Research Center for the People and the Press website. A November 26, 2012, article at Pew reported that in the 2012 election, Barack Obama won among voters under thirty by twenty-four points (60 percent to 36 percent), a huge margin, though less than his 2008 margin, which was thirty-four points. Obama actually lost among voters over thirty (48 percent to 50 percent). Obama's strength among millennials thus could be seen as giving victory to the Democratic Party.

Some commenters have argued that the Democratic advantage among millennials is overstated. For instance, Kirsten Powers in a March 19, 2014, article in *USA Today* argues that millennials are especially adaptable and unlikely to stay with one political party. Powers quotes a report by Third Way, a centrist Democratic think tank, which claims that millennials are "less likely to be satisfied with two static choices, and more apt to be swayed to change their tune." Thus, millennials may be especially willing to change their vote, and Democrats should not necessarily count on their support in future years. This view is bolstered by poll numbers, according to Aaron Stern in a March 26, 2014, article in the *Wall Street Journal*, which show that support for Democrats among millennials has dropped considerably. Stern says that in 2009 "nearly 50 percent of young voters viewed Democrats favorably." In March 2014, only 36 percent did, a drop of fourteen points.

Ron Fournier in a March 24, 2014, article in *National Journal* suggested that millennials are disenchanted with both Democrats and Republicans. "My generation had just two options politically—Democrats or Republicans, and that made sense to us. To my kids' generation, binary choices are absurd, especially when the choices are bad, which is why the two major parties are in danger of losing the future," Fournier says. Fournier suggests that millennials' independence may force both parties to adapt, or pave the way for a third party.

The following chapter examines Democrats' relationship with other important voting groups, including labor unions, minorities, and women.

> *"Breaking with the Democrats is long overdue. And once this is done, union members will likely choose the path taken by labor unions in nearly every developed country: the creation of a labor party, with its own platform, funding, and member activists."*

Labor Unions Should Abandon the Democratic Party Because of Its Right-Wing Policies

Shamus Cooke

Shamus Cooke is a social service worker, trade unionist, and writer for Workers Action. In the following viewpoint, he argues that the Democrats have completely abandoned labor unions and now represent the interests of the wealthy and of corporations. He points to Democratic attacks on public sector unions, and Barack Obama's education policy, which he says targets, scapegoats, and weakens teachers' unions. Cooke says union leaders are afraid to abandon Democrats and misinform members by telling them that the Democrats are pro-labor. Cooke concludes that unions need to stop giving donations to Demo-crats and instead should focus on building their own labor party to fight for workers' rights and interests.

As you read, consider the following questions:

1. What policies of Bill Clinton does Cooke say were anti-union?

2. According to Cooke, why is it dangerous for union leaders to praise Democrats in public when they know Democratic policies are anti-union?

3. What programs does Cooke say that a pro-labor political party should endorse?

The Democratic Party's participation in the recent [2013] national "sequester" cuts [in which across-the-board cuts were made in government spending] is yet another big dent in their love affair with organized labor. But breakups are often a protracted process. Before a relationship ends, there is usually a gradual deterioration based on irreconcilable differences, until the split becomes inevitable. The decades-long marriage of labor unions and the Democratic Party is nearing such a divorce. Labor unions are becoming frustrated as the Democrats flaunt their affair with corporate America and Wall Street.

The Divorce Process

What are some of the issues driving towards separation? It just seems that no matter how much labor leaders shower the politicians with money and affection, the Democrats just aren't returning the love.

Although the Democrats were always a fickle partner, their coldness evolved into aggression under Bill Clinton, who oversaw a slew of anti-worker legislation, most notably NAFTA [a free trade agreement with Mexico and Canada] and welfare "reform."

[Barack] Obama has continued this rightward trajectory, while portraying himself brilliantly as the "lesser evil" compared with the more honest anti-union rhetoric of the Republicans. He fulfilled none of his promises to labor in 2008, and essentially ignored all labor issues in his 2012 campaign. Labor leaders misinterpreted Obama as playing "hard to get," when in fact the Democratic Party had already moved on.

To prove his fidelity to his new crush, Wall Street, Obama has made it a pet project to target the most powerful union in the country—the teachers' union—for destruction. Obama's innocent-sounding Race to the Top education reform is in actuality an anti-union dismembering of public education, with its promotion of charter schools and its mass closings of public high schools that Obama labels as "failing." [George W.] Bush Jr.'s anti-union No Child Left Behind looks innocent compared to Obama's education "reform."

In fact, Obama has overseen the worst environment for organized labor since Ronald Reagan. But the problem is bigger than Obama. It's the entire Democratic Party. For example, Democratic governors across the United States continue to work in tandem with Republicans in weakening public employee unions—the last bastion of real strength in the labor movement.

The Democrats have chosen to blame labor unions for the economic crisis and the consequent budget deficits affecting the states. These deficits have been used to attack the wages, health care, and pensions of public employees on a state-by-state basis, fundamentally weakening these unions while skewing the labor market in favor of the employers.

What some labor leaders fail to understand is that political parties like the Democrats are centralized organizations that share certain beliefs and execute these ideas in a united fashion. It isn't merely a coincidence that every Democratic governor in the United States has chosen a similar anti-labor path as its policy. There has been a fundamental shift in the Democratic Party's relation to labor unions, and it is on display for everyone to see.

NEA Under Attack

Not all labor leaders are feigning blindness to these facts. The president of the nation's largest teachers' union, Dennis Van Roekel, summarized teachers' experience with the Obama administration:

"Today our members face the most anti-educator, anti-union, anti-student environment I have ever experienced." He was referring largely to Obama's above-mentioned Race to the Top education program.

Van Roekel's union, the National Education Association (NEA), also passed an excellent resolution at their national convention blasting Obama's education secretary, Arne Duncan, for his anti–public education and anti-union policies.

But of course Arne Duncan is simply implementing the policies of his boss, President Obama. And Obama is simply implementing the policies of his boss, corporate America, which is insisting that market relations are imposed on public education. After passing the above resolution, the NEA leadership shamefully pressured its membership to campaign for the Obama administration, akin to a survivor of domestic violence going to bat for the batterer.

The president of the large national public employee union American Federation of State, County and Municipal Employees (AFSCME), Lee Saunders, also lashed out against the Democrats recently:

> I am sick and tired of the fair-weather Democrats. They date us, take us to the prom, marry us, and then divorce us right after the honeymoon. I am sick and tired of the so-called friends who commend us when they're running for election, but condemn us after they've won. I am sick and tired

Obama, Teachers, and Unions

When candidate [Barack] Obama told the 2008 NEA [National Education Association, or the national teachers' union] national convention that he supported merit pay, getting rid of "bad teachers," and more charter schools, his remarks barely made a dent in the huge and orchestrated elect-Obama pep rally on the convention floor. Then NEA president Reg Weaver had warmed up the 10,000 delegates for Obama's speech by leading chants of "O! O! O!" from the podium. A few delegates booed Obama's remarks (that, after all, was what Obama wanted—he was "getting tough" with teachers' unions), and then the delegates resumed the pep rally, with groups of teachers snake dancing through the aisles in t-shirts announcing NEA's support for Obama's election.

The next morning, I walked into the California caucus to hear California Teachers Association (CTA) president David Sanchez and executive director Carolyn Doggett criticize Obama's speech. They told the delegates that Obama and his advisers were taking California for granted and were unresponsive to the point of being insulting. Sanchez and Doggett emphasized that Obama's education policies were at odds with NEA's opposition to merit pay. The CTA leadership threatened to pull out all stops to pressure Obama—but in the same breath pledged that CTA's support for Obama in the presidential race was unconditional, because "there is just no alternative."

Jack Gershon, "The New Corporate Agenda: Austerity, 'Shared Sacrifice' and Union Busting," in Todd Alan Price, John Duffy and Tania Giordani, eds. Defending Public Education from Corporate Takeover. Lanham, MD: University Press of America, 2012.

of the politicians who stand with us behind closed
doors, but kick us to the curb in front of the cam-
eras. I'm here to tell you that's bullshit and we're
not gonna take it anymore.

Accurate remarks, but they were limited to a couple of select Democratic mayors and governors. Again, there is more
than a "few bad apple" Democrats who are anti-labor; the
whole party is sick with this cancer.

In private, all labor leaders acknowledge this fact. Politico
reports:

Top labor leaders excoriated President Barack
Obama and Senate Majority Leader Harry Reid in a
closed session of the AFL-CIO's [American Federation of Labor and Congress of Industrial Organiza-
tions] executive board meeting.... Furious union
presidents complained about budget cuts, a new
[free] trade agreement and what some view as their
abandonment, even by their typically reliable allies
among Senate Democrats.

Presidents of several unions and an AFL-CIO
spokesman declined to repeat their private criticism
to a reporter Tuesday, a sign that labor feels it must
still try to maintain a relationship with the Democratic Party, even if it's deeply troubled.

So while the presidents of these unions speak honestly
amongst themselves, they feel obligated to mis-educate their
membership about the above facts. Labor leaders consistently
minimize the Democrats' role in anti-union policies, while ex-
aggerating any morsel that can be construed to be pro-union.
A mis-educated union membership makes for a weakened
union movement.

Lying to Members

When President Obama gave a largely right-wing State of the
Union address that included more corporate free trade agree-

ments, more education "reform," cuts to Medicare, and no plan to address the ongoing jobs crisis, AFL-CIO president Richard Trumka responded shamefully by saying:

> Tonight, President Obama sent a clear message to the world that he will stand and fight for working America's values and priorities.

Again, Trumka knows better. He should tell union members the truth. The AFL-CIO and other unions have lied about President Obama's role in the national "sequester" cuts, blaming the whole thing on the Republicans. The truth, however, is that Obama formed "the deficit reduction committee" that gave birth to the sequester. He failed to take any significant action to prevent the cuts, because he agrees with them.

Rank-and-file union members aren't stupid. They realize it when their paychecks shrink, when their health care costs skyrocket, when their pensions are destroyed, when they're laid off, or when they campaign for Democrats who betray them post-election. Union leaders are creating distrust within their membership as they continue down a political road that has left labor weakened and politically tied to a "partner" that's abusing it.

The Democrats have gone "all in" with Wall Street and the corporations. The big banks now feel as comfortable throwing campaign donations towards the Democrats as the Republicans. Labor unions can't compete with Wall Street's cash.

Breaking with the Democrats is long overdue. And once this is done, union members will likely choose the path taken by labor unions in nearly every developed country: the creation of a labor party, with its own platform, funding, and member activists.

Such a party could appeal directly to all working people by demanding that a federal jobs program be immediately implemented to put those unemployed to work as well as fighting to save and expand Social Security and Medicare, while taxing the rich and corporations to fully fund public education and other social services. Such a platform would create a massive contrast to the mainstream corporate-bought parties that exist today, and thus attract millions of members and millions more voters.

"Union members—it is time to break the allegiance with the Democratic Party."

Labor Unions Should Abandon the Democratic Party Because of Its Left-Wing Policies

Chad Stafko

Chad Stafko is a writer and political consultant. In the following viewpoint, he argues that unions should support Republicans since union members agree with Republicans on key issues. In particular, he says that union members dislike Barack Obama's health reform initiative and that they oppose immigration, which Democrats support. Stafko also blames Obama for the poor economy, which he says has hurt union members.

As you read, consider the following questions:

1. Why is Joseph Hansen angry at Obama, and what does he say his union will do in 2014?

2. What did a Rasmussen poll that Stafko cites find out about union support for immigration reform?

3. According to Stafko, how did average weekly earnings of union members change over Obama's first term?

For generations the Democratic Party has relied upon unions and their members to dutifully pull the lever for Democratic candidates and to man their call centers and canvass neighborhoods. And yet, an objective look at what are arguably the three biggest issues shows that Democrats are on the wrong side of these issues when compared to the desires and needs of union members.

Union members—it is time to break the allegiance with the Democratic Party.

Obamacare

Take the issue of Obamacare [referring to the Patient Protection and Affordable Care Act, also known as the Affordable Care Act]. According to a *Wall Street Journal*/NBC News poll conducted May 30–June 2, 49% of respondents believe Obamacare to be a bad idea, while only 37% see the Affordable Care Act as beneficial. That 49% is the highest rating since polling began on the issue back in March 2010, indicating that support is eroding for the much ballyhooed legislation.

The poll also found that twice as many individuals believe they will be worse off under Obamacare than better off. That belief is especially strong among those who receive their health care insurance through the government or an employer—a description that fits many union workers.

Expecting to be worse off under Obamacare is synonymous with the common belief that you will pay more for your health care benefits under Obamacare or that your employer will drop the employer-sponsored health care plan.

Even union leaders, many of whom originally pushed hard for the law and encouraged members to support the legislation, have been barking at President Obama of late as to the negative effect Obamacare will have on its members.

Joseph Hansen, president of the 1.3 million-member United Food and Commercial Workers International Union, recently opined in an op-ed for the *Hill* newspaper that the union will withdraw support of Democrats in 2014 if Obama isn't able to deliver on his promise, made in 2009, that union members could keep their existing insurance. Hansen wrote, "The President's statement to labor in 2009 is simply not true for millions of workers."

In other words, Hansen is saying that Obama, [House Minority Leader Nancy] Pelosi, and the rest of the Democrat gang lied to the unions—and therefore the union members— regarding what would happen to them under Obamacare so as to gain their support to get the legislation passed. As a union member, why would you then vote for someone in the next election who essentially looked you square in the eyes and lied to you?

Other unions have shown similar angst. The Teamsters [the International Brotherhood of Teamsters union], along with an established hotel workers' union, have sought substantial changes to the Affordable Care Act. The president of the United Union of Roofers, Waterproofers, and Allied Workers released a statement in April [2013] calling for the repeal or complete reform of the Affordable Care Act.

These statements sound more like those made by Republican legislators back in 2010 when they fought unsuccessfully, as the minority party, to block Obamacare.

Union members would be wise to recall that it will be these same Democrats who conjured up this massive deceit of union members who will have their hands out in 2014 and beyond, expecting union members to dutifully vote for and support them.

Immigration Reform

Immigration reform is another issue of which the Democrats are on the wrong side of the issue versus union members. A

Rasmussen poll taken earlier this year found that 90% of union members felt the issue was important to them with 51% of union respondents indicating that they opposed amnesty for illegal immigrants.

Granted, 51% is only a slight majority. However, consider that a near unanimous number of Democrats support some version of amnesty.

Union members are right to oppose amnesty from an economic perspective. Amnesty would result in millions of suddenly legal workers who could latch on to non-union labor groups and give organizations in need of labor a far lower cost alternative to consider.

Democrats don't care about that. All they see is that suddenly legal immigrants will soon be loyal voting Democrats for decades to come. Given that the estimate is that there would be a potential 11 million new citizens as the result of amnesty and that total U.S. union membership has fallen to only 14.4 million, and declining still, Democrats could soon forget all that labor unions and their members have done for them in the past decades.

The Economy

The third issue union members should consider in abandoning their allegiance to Democrats is the state of the economy and its effect on them. Average weekly earnings of union members was $943 in 2012. Back in 2009, Obama's first year in office, union workers earned $908 per week. Compounded over three years, that results in a scant 1.27% growth rate in union members' earnings.

As a comparison, during President George W. Bush's final four years in office, wages of union workers grew an average of 3.19% per year, about two and a half times the rate under Obama.

The weak Obama economy has also contributed to an overall U.S. union membership that is now at its lowest level since the 1930s. A weakened economy has resulted in less tax revenues filtering into state government coffers. In the case of cash-strapped states, this has produced layoffs and/or furloughs of government workers, many of whom are union members.

Added to the weak wage growth of union members during the last several years are the tax increases under Obama that have certainly affected union members and their families. When you consider the tax increases coupled with the anemic growth in wages along with the effects of inflation, in many cases union members have likely seen a decrease in their disposable income.

From Obamacare, to immigration reform, to the weak economy, Democrats from Congress to the White House have failed union members.

"As the Republican Party begins a process of soul-searching to determine why it has such difficulty making inroads among minority populations, it may want to start by looking at the long-range economic effects of its policies."

Minorities Vote for Democrats Because They Do Better with Democratic Policies

Zoltan Hajnal and Jeremy D. Horowitz

Zoltan Hajnal, coauthor of Why Americans Don't Join the Party: Race, Immigration, and the Failure (of Political Parties) to Engage the Electorate, *is a professor of political science at the University of California (UC), San Diego. Jeremy D. Horowitz is a UC San Diego political science doctoral student. In the following viewpoint, the authors argue that economic data show that minority groups, including African Americans, Hispanics, and Asian Americans, experience much more economic improvement under Democrats than under Republicans. This improvement does not come at the expense of whites, whose economic standing also improves among Democratic administrations. The authors*

*say the improvements could be a result of policies targeted at re-
ducing poverty or at reducing racial inequities. In any case, the
authors conclude, minorities who vote for Democrats are doing
so based on the correct belief that Democratic policies will improve their lives.*

As you read, consider the following questions:

1. What data do the authors cite to show that African
   American economic standing improved under Democratic presidents?

2. According to the authors, what happens to minority
   fortunes the longer Democrats stay in office?

3. What antipoverty programs do the authors say may have
   improved the fortunes of minorities under Democratic
   administrations?

Speaking to donors after the election, Mitt Romney attrib-
uted his loss to President [Barack] Obama to the
administration's strategy of "giving a lot of stuff" to blacks
and Latinos, citing in particular "free healthcare" and "amnesty for the children of illegals." But data show a more plausible explanation: Black, Latino and Asian American voters,
who overwhelmingly voted for Obama, were simply evaluating
the long-term record of each party.

Minorities Gain Under Democrats

The data we analyzed show unequivocally that minorities fare
better under Democratic administrations than under Republican ones. Census data tracking annual changes in income,
poverty and unemployment over the last five decades tell a
striking story about the relationship between the president's
party and minority well-being.

Under Democratic presidents, the incomes of black families grew by an average of $895 a year, but only by $142 a year

under Republicans. Across 26 years of Democratic leadership, unemployment among blacks declined by 7.9%; under 28 years of Republican presidencies, the rate increased by a net of 13.7%. Similarly, the black poverty rate fell by 23.6% under Democratic presidents and rose by 3% under Republicans.

The results for Latinos and Asians, though based on fewer years of data, show the same pattern. For example, Latino incomes grew an average of $627 a year under Democrats and fell by $197 a year under Republicans. The data similarly show that the living standards of Asian Americans have improved under Democrats and stagnated under Republicans.

More important, these gains do not come at the expense of whites. On average, white incomes have similarly grown, and white joblessness and poverty have likewise declined, under Democratic administrations. These numbers show that economic conditions need not be a zero-sum game pitting races and ethnicities against one another.

Some might argue that Democrats have been lucky enough to preside during more prosperous times or, indeed, have simply benefited from the long-term results of Republican fiscal policies. In three ways, however, the data suggest that this is not the case, and instead point to a real and substantial partisan divergence.

First, even accounting for the overall state of the economy and other longer-term trends in well-being, partisan differences persist. When controlling for inflation and changes in the gross national product, and accounting for other factors such as oil prices and the proportion of adults in the workforce, we find similarly large gains for minorities under Democrats and equally sharp losses under Republicans.

Second, these partisan trends are remarkably consistent. Black incomes grew in 77% of the years under Democratic control, while black poverty and unemployment declined 88% and 71%, respectively. In sharp contrast, blacks lost more often than not under Republican administrations.

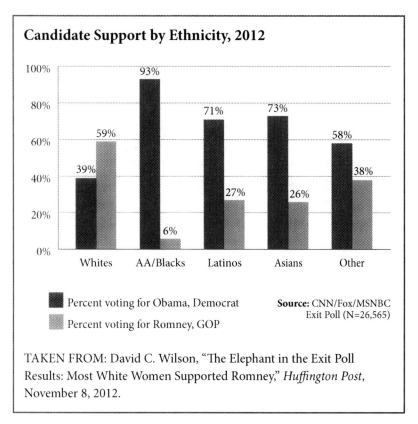

Candidate Support by Ethnicity, 2012

- Percent voting for Obama, Democrat
- Percent voting for Romney, GOP

Source: CNN/Fox/MSNBC Exit Poll (N=26,565)

TAKEN FROM: David C. Wilson, "The Elephant in the Exit Poll Results: Most White Women Supported Romney," *Huffington Post*, November 8, 2012.

Finally, the longer Democratic administrations are in office, the more they appear to help blacks and other minorities experience economic gains. As Republican presidents stay in office longer, however, the fortunes of minority groups increasingly suffer.

Potential Explanations

Policy differences between the parties offer many potential explanations for the minority gains. Initiatives intended to boost the incomes and employment of lower-income Americans, such as Lyndon Johnson's "War on Poverty" or Bill Clinton's expansion of the earned income tax credit, certainly could play a role. So could more racially targeted efforts, such as the Civil Rights Act and initiatives to expand affirmative action in government hiring.

A range of other policies, such as education and immigration efforts, might especially benefit minority communities. And policies that encourage overall economic and job growth, which Democratic presidents tend to emphasize more than their GOP counterparts, can make a positive difference for minorities—along with everyone else.

Minorities are becoming an increasingly large segment of the electorate. As the Republican Party begins a process of soul-searching to determine why it has such difficulty making inroads among minority populations, it may want to start by looking at the long-range economic effects of its policies.

> *"Democrats have done little for blacks in decades that has resulted in meaningful and measurable results, all while pocketing their votes."*

An Inconvenient Truth: Neither Party Is Serious About Diversity

Ron Christie

Ron Christie is chief executive officer of Christie Strategies, a media and political strategy firm. He previously served as special assistant to President George W. Bush and deputy assistant to Vice President Dick Cheney from 2001 to 2004. He has written three books on race and politics in America. In the following viewpoint, he argues that Democrats have not done much for African American voters, since unemployment rates remain high and the economy is poor. He says that Republicans need to improve their communication with African American groups by touting school vouchers and other programs that will help blacks and distinguish Republicans from Democrats.

As you read, consider the following questions:

1. What point does Christie grudgingly concede?

2. According to Christie, what facts show that Democrats aren't worried about losing African American votes?

3. What is the Republican motive for voter ID laws, according to Christie?

I read with interest Jamelle Bouie's piece this week—"Racism Not a Problem Anymore? Don't Be Ridiculous, It's Still a Big Issue." Yes, there are unenlightened people in this country who will discriminate based on skin color. But let's also confront another inconvenient truth: America's major political parties aren't serious about meaningful diversity either.

Failure to Communicate

Democrats have done little for blacks in decades that has resulted in meaningful and measurable results, all while pocketing their votes. Republicans have fumbled at nearly every opportunity to make significant inroads in communities of color because, with few exceptions, they simply don't know how to effectively communicate a compelling vision.

Since the 1960s, blacks have clung to the Democratic Party—the same party that imposed segregation and fought passage of the Civil Rights Act of 1964 and the Voting Rights Act of 1965. Democrats have created the myth that Republicans have sought to inhibit the progress of blacks at every turn, a fiction that Republicans have been unable to combat due to their inability to communicate effectively.

Critics will rebut this assertion with the charge that it was southern Democrats who largely sought to block the civil rights programs—many of whom would change their allegiance to the Republican Party. Fair enough. This point I will grudgingly concede.

However, it was not the Party of Lincoln that illegally wiretapped the phone of Martin Luther King Jr.; we have then attorney general Robert F. Kennedy and FBI [Federal Bureau of Investigation] director J. Edgar Hoover to thank for that. It was the Party of Lincoln that found enough votes to propel the Great Society programs over the finish line to deliver victory for President Lyndon B. Johnson, who infamously declared in regard to these measures: "I'll have those n-----s voting Democratic for the next 200 years."

Whether Johnson's motives to bring about a Great Society were ulterior or altruistic in nature, one aspect rings true for me today: for all the trillions of dollars spent to ameliorate poverty, provide job training and assistance during economic downturns, the unemployment rate for blacks has remained much the same for the past 50 years.

Black Unemployment

In a powerful report published this year by the Economic Policy Institute, author Algernon Austin notes: "... The average unemployment rate for blacks over the past 50 years, at 11.6 percent, is considerably higher than the average rate during recessions of 6.7 percent." Even worse, Austin noted that over the last 50 years, the black unemployment rate remained at a level either even or *higher* than during a typical recession.

The fact that black unemployment in America rose from 13.4 percent to 14.3 percent in October 2012 and President Obama still received 93 percent of the black vote tells you Democrats aren't worried about losing this key bloc, despite little meaningful progress on unemployment or upward mobility.

President Kennedy's charge to support tax reform with the famous phrase "a rising tide lifts all boats" is one that rings as true today as it was when he said it in 1963. Kennedy believed that higher participation in the economy would *strengthen* the economy. Decades of programs focused on wealth distribution

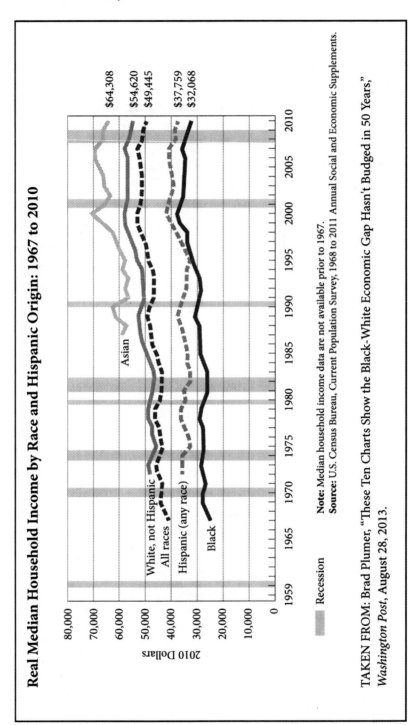

Real Median Household Income by Race and Hispanic Origin: 1967 to 2010

$64,308
$54,620
$49,445
$37,759
$32,068

Asian

White, not Hispanic
All races

Hispanic (any race)

Black

2010 Dollars

Recession

Note: Median household income data are not available prior to 1967.
Source: U.S. Census Bureau, Current Population Survey, 1968 to 2011 Annual Social and Economic Supplements.

TAKEN FROM: Brad Plumer, "These Ten Charts Show the Black-White Economic Gap Hasn't Budged in 50 Years," *Washington Post*, August 28, 2013.

and government dependency have largely proven ineffective in enacting significant change to the upward mobility of many communities of color. If only President Obama had echoed this note yesterday [in December 2013] in his speech regarding income inequality—an opportunity missed.

Despite this dismal track record, Republicans haven't made significant inroads with communities of color. Part of this is due to the stigma many black Democrats perpetuate in that voting for Republicans is the sign of one being a sellout or traitor to their race. A larger part of the problem is that the GOP "big thinkers" haven't had a clue about how to actually communicate why our policies, vision, and ideology deserve a closer look.

A New Message

Following the 2012 presidential election, the Republican National Committee issued a self-flagellating report that missed the real root causes of low minority turnout for the GOP—all at the cost of several million dollars. Seriously, I could have told them for free.

For one, the GOP needs to realize that there is no monolithic way of thinking in black America. For too long, the voices of [civil rights activists] Al Sharpton and Jesse Jackson have scared Republicans into believing otherwise. While there is still inequality in America, the civil rights era is over. GOP outreach must extend beyond churches and congregations.

Next, stop treating black people like black people. All blacks aren't poor, on welfare, or in jail. Articulating a strong pro-growth message that is anchored in the bedrock of a strong education would be a nice place to start.

While Obama's Department of Justice is busy suing Louisiana in an attempt to deny the ability of largely poor black children to escape failing schools under the rubric of diversity, Republicans should trumpet the success of school-choice programs. More than half of black men without a high school diploma are unemployed today; this situation will not improve until black children are not castigated for "acting white" by trying to learn in school. And in case you were wondering, both the attorney general and the president send their children to private school.

Moreover, Republicans should explain how they seek to treat all Americans equally under the law rather than curry special favor based on race and/or ethnicity. Despite all the cries of Democrats that Republicans are seeking to disenfranchise black voters by imposing strict voter ID requirements, nothing could be further from the truth. In fact, the number of blacks who voted in states such as Indiana and Georgia after voter ID [identification] laws were imposed *increased*, rather than declined.

Democratic Paternalism

The paternalistic notion that blacks are not capable of obtaining an ID tells you plenty about what many Democrats think of blacks in the 21st century. Given that one cannot board a train, plane, purchase alcohol, or enter Eric Holder's Department of Justice without an ID, I suspect ulterior motives may be at play, an approach more about keeping and obtaining power at whatever the cost.

Finally, the incubator for success for Republicans will ultimately be found by looking at past electoral results as a beacon for future success. Before 1900, none of the 23 blacks elected to Congress were Democrats. The first black elected to the United States Senate? Ed Brooke from Massachusetts. In an interview with the Daily Beast last year, Brooke offered counsel that national Republicans should listen to. In the relevant passage, the former senator, now 92, noted:

> My father was a Republican. My mother was a Republican. They wouldn't dare be a Democrat. The Democrats were a party opposed to civil rights. The

South was all Democratic conservatives. And the African-American community considered them the enemy.

Times have changed. Many Democrats from the 1800s to the mid-20th century represented the party of Dixie and the Confederacy. The sad irony is that President Johnson, himself a southern Democrat, was ostensibly supportive of the Civil Rights and Voting Acts . . . while his private comments reveal a different posture. Barry Goldwater, his opponent in 1964, opposed these programs, leading to the near unanimous shift of blacks to form a lockstep allegiance with the Democratic Party. An opportunity seized upon by Democrats then and now—an opportunity wasted by Republicans for 50 years and one that we can change if we can offer a compelling path forward. The time to act is now.

So while race and racism remain in America today, it is clear both of our major political parties are stuck in neutral on how best to address diversity. Democrats take a certain voting bloc for granted because they can and Republicans' woes are largely due to self-inflicted wounds. This is not the color-blind America Dr. King and true leaders of the civil rights era fought for. We can and must do better.

> "The fact that the gender gap persists
> not only across age groups, but within
> major racial, ethnic, and marital-status
> groups reinforces the conclusion that a
> gender difference in political orienta-
> tion is a fundamental part of today's
> American political and social scene."

Women More Likely to Be Democrats, Regardless of Age

Frank Newport

*Frank Newport is Gallup's editor in chief, and he is past presi-
dent of the American Association for Public Opinion Research.
In the following viewpoint, he presents survey results showing
that women are more likely to identify as Democrats than are
men and less likely than men to identify as Independents; Republican identification of men and women is close to even. The
greater identification of women with Democrats is consistent
across age and ethnic groups. Newport concludes that gender differences are central to partisan identification in the United
States.*

As you read, consider the following questions:

1. According to the survey, what percentage of women identify as Democrats, Independents, and Republicans? What percentage of men?

2. Which groups are most Democratic in orientation among whites, blacks, and Asians?

3. How does marital status affect Democratic identification, according to the survey?

A new Gallup analysis of almost 150,000 interviews conducted from January through May of this year [2009] sheds new light on the substantial gender gap that exists in American politics today. Not only are women significantly more likely than men to identify as Democrats, and less likely to identify as Independents, but—with only slight variation—this gap is evident across all ages, from 18 to 85, and within all major racial, ethnic, and marital-status segments of society.

A recent Gallup analysis confirmed the existence of a fundamental gender gap in American political party identification today, although the exact nature of that gap has varied over recent years. The major distinction in political party identification today seems to revolve around the percentage of each gender who identify as Democrats versus Independents; men and women have been similar in terms of identification with the Republican Party this year.

In the current analysis of 149,192 Gallup poll daily tracking interviews conducted in January through May of this year, 41% of women identify as Democrats, some nine points higher than the 32% of men who identify as Democrats. The 34% of men in this sample who are Independents can be contrasted with the smaller 26% of women who are Independents. There is little difference by gender in terms of identification as Republicans—28% of men are Republicans, compared to 25% of women.

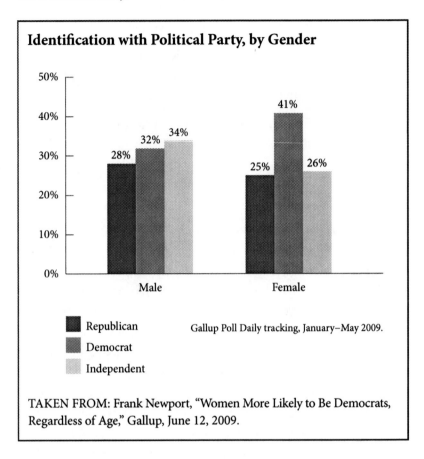

Identification with Political Party, by Gender

Republican
Democrat
Independent

Gallup Poll Daily tracking, January–May 2009.

TAKEN FROM: Frank Newport, "Women More Likely to Be Democrats, Regardless of Age," Gallup, June 12, 2009.

Overall, the data confirm that men currently have a much more even distribution of party identification than do women. The range across the three partisan groups for men is just 6 points, from a low of 28% identifying as Republicans to a high of 34% identifying as Independents. On the other hand, the range for women is a much larger 16 points, from 25% Republican to 41% Democratic.

The Age Factor

Previous Gallup research has shown significant variations in party identification across age groups in the American population. Baby boomers (aged 45–63) are more likely than average to identify as Democrats, as are younger Americans in

Generation Y (aged 18–29), while Generation X (aged 30–44) as well as older Americans are somewhat more Republican in orientation. The new Gallup analysis, importantly, shows the persistence of a gender gap not only within each of these broad age groups, but at every age, from 18 to 85, even as the overall party identification patterns shift across the age spectrum. . . .

The broad trends certainly document the fact that the Democratic over Republican advantage varies across age groups. Democrats have their greatest advantage among baby boomers and the very young, and are weakest, relatively speaking, among those in their late 30s and in their mid to late 60s. *The key point for the current analysis, however, is that these variations occur among both men and women.* There is, as noted, a gender gap in this partisan orientation measure at every age point, from 18 to 85. . . .

The gender gap is largest in terms of Democratic and Independent identification, and smallest for the percentage identifying as Republicans, but for the most part, a gender gap exists for every age in terms of each of these three partisan groups.

Racial and Ethnic Groups

There are well-known and significant differences in the patterns of partisan identification across major racial and ethnic groups. Blacks and Asians are more Democratic in orientation than are whites (blacks, much more so). But within each of these three groups, women are more Democratic than men.

Overall, Hispanics (of any race) are more Democratic than non-Hispanics. But Hispanic women are more Democratic in orientation than Hispanic men, and non-Hispanic women are more Democratic than non-Hispanic men.

Marital Status

There are also significant differences in Democratic orientation within segments of Americans based on their marital status. In general, Americans who are living with a domestic partner, those who are separated but not divorced, and those who are single are more Democratic than others. Married Americans are the least likely to be Democrats. But, as was the case for racial and ethnic groups, the data show a gender gap within each of these groups. Single women are more Democratic than single men, married women are more Democratic than married men, divorced women are more Democratic than divorced men, and so forth.

Implications

Although the existence of a gender gap in American politics has been well established, the very large sample sizes available with Gallup poll daily tracking allow for a more-detailed-than-normal examination of the nature of gender differences. The remarkable finding is that women of all ages are more Democratic in orientation than are men of the same ages, and that women of all ages are also less likely than men of the same ages to be Independent. (The differences by age in the percentage identifying as Republican are much smaller.)

This means that whatever forces are at work that determine party identification in America today—socialization, cultural patterns, social position, social status, and life orientation—are already in place by the time young men and women reach the age of 18. And, these same patterns seem to have affected or are currently affecting men and women in their 80s in a similar fashion. The fact that the gender gap persists not only across age groups, but within major racial, ethnic, and marital-status groups reinforces the conclusion that a gender difference in political orientation is a fundamental part of today's American political and social scene.

Survey Methods

Results are based on telephone interviews with 149,192 national adults, aged 18 and older, conducted Jan. 2–May 31,

2009, as part of Gallup poll daily tracking. For results based on the total sample of national adults, one can say with 95% confidence that the maximum margin of sampling error is ±1 percentage points.

Interviews are conducted with respondents on landline telephones (for respondents with a landline telephone) and cellular phones (for respondents who are cell phone only).

In addition to sampling error, question wording and practical difficulties in conducting surveys can introduce error or bias into the findings of public opinion polls.

> "The skepticism runs especially deep among blue-collar women, sometimes known as 'waitress moms,' whose deeply pessimistic attitudes toward the Affordable Care Act should riddle Democratic candidates with anxiety."

Democrats Are Struggling with Women Voters

Alex Roarty

Alex Roarty is the chief political correspondent for National Journal Hotline. *In the following viewpoint, he reports on poll results showing that white women have an especially negative view of Barack Obama's health care reform initiative, the Patient Protection and Affordable Care Act, also known as Obamacare. Roarty argues that Democrats are especially dependent on white women voters in congressional elections. He concludes that the unpopularity of Obamacare may badly damage Democrats in congressional races.*

As you read, consider the following questions:

1. Why does Roarty believe Democrats will have to fight to retain core elements of their constituency?

2. What do poll numbers show about the attitudes of white women without a higher education toward the health care law?

3. Who is Mark Begich, and why does Roarty believe the polls are bad news for him?

It's not the voters who hate Obamacare [referring to the Patient Protection and Affordable Care Act, also known as the Affordable Care Act (ACA)] the most who are going to matter in next year's elections. It's the Independents who frequently side with Democrats but could, if propelled by a distaste for the health care law, take a serious look at the GOP in 2014. And on this front, Democrats have a big problem with one of their most crucial constituencies—white women.

Skeptical About Obamacare

Polling provided to *National Journal* by the Kaiser Family Foundation shows that white women have soured considerably on the law, especially in the month since its botched rollout. The skepticism runs especially deep among blue-collar women, sometimes known as "waitress moms," whose deeply pessimistic attitudes toward the Affordable Care Act should riddle Democratic candidates with anxiety.

Certainly, the law's unpopularity gives Republicans a tool to counter the Democratic claim of a GOP "war on women"—something Republicans failed miserably at in 2012. But more significantly, it demonstrates that Democrats will have to fight just to retain core elements of their constituency. With 2014's most important campaigns already lying in hostile territory like Alaska, Arkansas, and South Dakota, it's a battle many of these candidates can ill afford.

The Kaiser poll, which has been conducted monthly since Obamacare's inception, shows the law has never been a big hit with white women. But this group's opinions took a sharply negative turn in the November results.

According to Kaiser, 40 percent of college-educated white women hold a "very unfavorable" view of the law—10 points higher than a month ago. An additional 10 percent view the law "somewhat unfavorably." A month ago, those two groups together totaled just 42 percent.

That's not damning in and of itself, but this is the one slice of the white electorate where Democrats usually perform well. President Obama won 46 percent of the group in 2012, and even that was an underwhelming showing compared with recent Democratic presidential candidates.

Women and Health Care Concerns

And that's not all. Democrats should be far more worried about white women who do not have a higher education. The numbers are astounding: In the latest Kaiser poll, 50 percent have a "very unfavorable" view of the law—9 points higher than in October. An additional 13 percent view it "somewhat unfavorably." Indeed, antipathy among blue-collar white women runs even deeper than the most conservative white demographic group, blue-collar white men (59 percent of whom hold an unfavorable view, Kaiser found).

Remarkably, only 16 percent of blue-collar white women have a favorable view of Obamacare. They disapprove of it by a 4–1 ratio. (The poll found 21 percent did not know enough about the ACA to hold an opinion.) These voters are by no means a strongly Democratic group: Obama won just 39 percent of them last year. But they do lean further left than their male counterparts, and Democratic candidates in 2014 will need to perform even better with them to win reelection. In 2008, for example, Democrat Mark Begich won his Senate race in Alaska by claiming 54 percent of the white female vote, which constituted 41 percent of the state's electorate. He's a top GOP target in 2014.

Republicans suggest that white women's deep pessimism is rooted in the cascade of negative media surrounding the law.

"Women are more interested in having health care than men are," said Keith Emis, an Arkansas-based GOP pollster who works for Rep. Tom Cotton, the likely Republican challenger to Democratic Sen. Mark Pryor. "They have paid a whole lot more attention to this."

Obamacare's unpopularity runs deep in other Democratic constituencies too. A new poll by Harvard's Institute of Politics, for one, found millennials [those born roughly in the 1990s and later] turning away from the law. And some GOP pollsters argue that focusing on the effects of just one group is misguided. "This isn't just small segments of the electorate; these are huge, broad topics that affect everybody," said David Winston, a Republican pollster with close ties to the House GOP. "Who isn't interested in health care?"

But groups such as the millennials aren't as important to Democratic candidates like Begich and Pryor who are up for reelection. Women are crucial to their causes. And while Democrats might ultimately be able to sell voters on a "fix it, don't repeal it" approach to Obamacare, the data show they've still got a lot more work to do.

| *"The white working class has the potential to be a—if not the—decisive swing voter group for the future."*

Why the Democrats Still Need Working-Class White Voters

Andrew Levison and Ruy Teixeira

Andrew Levison is author of The White Working Class Today: Who They Are, How They Think and How Progressives Can Regain Their Support. *Ruy Teixeira is a senior fellow at the Center for American Progress and coauthor of* The Emerging Democratic Majority. *In the following viewpoint, they argue that Democrats need white working-class voters to consistently win presidential and congressional elections. They suggest that white working-class voters could be swayed to the Democratic Party with sustained grassroots organizing and a serious attempt to include the white working class in Democratic decision making.*

As you read, consider the following questions:

1. According to the authors, what damaged Republican standing with white working-class voters in 2012?

2. What percentage of white working-class voters need to be swayed in order to produce a two percentage point pro-Democratic shift?

3. How are Get Out the Vote (GOTV) efforts different from the kind of grassroots organizing the authors recommend?

In the months since the 2012 elections it has become apparent that the victorious Democratic coalition Obama assembled is still not sufficiently large to overcome the unprecedented Republican obstruction and sabotage of the normal processes of American political life.

Although long-term demographic trends, such as the increase in minority voters and the rise of the millennial generation, are favorable for the Democrats, translating those trends into true political and electoral dominance will remain difficult so long as Democrats rely on simply turning out core Obama coalition voters. Their margins will be too thin and subject to backlash, especially below the presidential level.

To create a stable Democratic majority, Democrats need to win the support of a significant group of voters who are now part of the Republican coalition. As the 2012 elections demonstrated, the group that has perhaps the greatest potential in this regard is the white working class.

Consider the following:

First, in terms of sheer size, even at 36 percent of voters (and that is the exit poll figure—the census data indicate a share about 8 points higher), the white working class remains one of the biggest sociologically distinct demographic groups that is now heavily part of the red state/GOP coalition.

Second, a significant number of white working-class voters have historic ties with the Democrats—even among those who currently vote Republican. Some have personal memories and other family traditions of past Democratic voting. No comparable connection or previous ideological affinity exists with today's upper income or other Republican voters.

As a result, on both the positive side and on the negative side, the white working class has the potential to be a—if not the—decisive swing voter group for the future. On the positive side, permanently increasing the level of Democratic support among white workers to just the 40 percent Obama received in 2008 (he received 36 percent in 2012) could actually ensure a genuinely stable and reliable Democratic majority for many years to come. On the negative side, if in 2016 white working-class support for the Dems falls to or below the 33 percent it hit in 2010, a GOP president becomes a very real possibility. Not to mention the dire effects such low support would have on Democratic prospects in 2014: It would be essentially impossible for Democrats to retake the House and they might well lose the Senate in the bargain.

In both 2008 and 2012, Obama and the Democrats were assisted by a strongly favorable combination of circumstances among white workers. In 2008 the financial crisis and a desire to "clean house" boosted white working-class support for Obama. In 2012, the GOP fielded a uniquely aloof and unsympathetic Republican candidate, Republican governors initiated a series of profoundly provocative and insulting actions in critical midwestern states and Republicans were not helped by the weak but nonetheless discernible economic recovery in the months before Election Day.

Democrats cannot count on these factors being repeated in the future; quite the contrary, the GOP, despite its intense ideological myopia, will not intentionally repeat exactly the same set of tactical and strategic mistakes it made in 2012. In 2016 GOP messaging will be far more focused on expressing concern for "the middle class" and "average Americans." Rhetorically attractive (but substantively vacuous) policy packages aimed at the middle class, like those recently offered by GOP

House minority leader Eric Cantor, will become a standard feature of GOP campaigns. Future contests will be harder, not easier.

Many Democrats' immediate reaction will be that the task of winning a greater share of the white working-class vote is hopeless; white workers' votes for Republicans simply reflect their deeply rooted "conservatism." But this confuses two related but distinct concepts: conservatism and cultural traditionalism. While white workers are overwhelmingly cultural traditionalists they are not all conservatives. Despite the well-entrenched clichés of "conservative white workers" the group is actually divided, depending on the issues, with majorities being "populist" on some issues and conservative on others.

But even more important, as shown in *The White Working Class Today*—a new book by Andrew Levison, a coauthor of this piece—a significant group of white workers who currently vote for the GOP are "open minded," not progressive but persuadable, on a wide range of issues including many traditionally associated with conservatives and the GOP. Such issues range from assistance for the poor and the need for government regulations to attitudes about social, ethnic and religious tolerance. Many white workers, while not Democrats, are also not Rush Limbaugh/FOX News conservatives.

This division suggests the outline of a strategy for building an expanded Democratic coalition: If the white working class currently represents 36 percent of the electorate, now split 62–36 between Republicans and Democrats (as per the 2012 exit poll), Republican-voting white workers represent 22 percent of voters. (Note that this assumes, as is prudent, that Democratic support among the white working class was not artificially depressed by the race of the candidate. Gore and Kerry in their losing efforts of 2000 and 2004 averaged very close to Obama's level of white working-class support across 2008 and 2012. National Democratic candidates, white or black, currently do very poorly among white working-class voters.)

If just 10 percent of the group that currently votes Republican is persuadable, a successful appeal for their votes would produce a 2 percentage point pro-Democratic shift in the electorate. This would have meant a 53 percent Democratic presidential tally in 2012, not 51 percent. This could be the critical margin of safety in presidential elections in 2016 and 2020.

Moreover it is not simply a matter of raw votes on Election Day. A 10 percent partisan shift among white workers would reduce the ideological hegemony that Republicans have in many white working-class communities. Even in red state areas of the country like the South, where Obama likely received around 24% of the white working-class vote (full data on the white working-class vote by state have not yet been released), a 10 percent shift could expand the limits of "acceptable" debate and subtly pressure candidates in now entirely conservative districts to shift slightly toward the center. In areas like the rust belt states of the Midwest, where Obama was likely more in the 42% range, it could provide critical margins for Democratic victory.

In order to successfully appeal to this critical group of voters, Democrats will need to do more than create a few clever TV ads or emphatically repeat Democratic campaign clichés left over from the 1950s.

The key is *representation*. As research by Democracy Corps has shown, more than anything else white working-class voters feel that neither party is really "looking out for them."

The perennial frustration Democrats experience in attempting to appeal to white working people is that programs they champion, ones that offer concrete social and economic benefits, are nonetheless viewed by these voters with profound suspicion and distrust. As the Democracy Corps research revealed, the essential problem is that, because white working-class voters do not feel they have any significant role or status within the Democratic coalition and community, they similarly feel no ownership or control over these programs' operation nor do they have any trust in their design. White working-class voters will only develop greater trust in Democratic programs and policies when they trust in the political party that designs them and feel a sense of representation in its operations.

The long-term solution, then, cannot be simply a new package of traditional Democratic programs and policies, promoted through TV ads. Rather, it will require the rebuilding of grassroots political organizations in white working-class communities across America, modern and more genuinely participatory versions of the traditional Democratic "machines."

Although often disparaged as simply cynical top-down institutions that delivered votes for Democratic candidates, at the neighborhood and precinct level local Democratic clubs were also a significant community service organization for urban working-class Americans—a source of municipal jobs for relatives and for intercession with the city and state bureaucracy when problems arose on issues like veterans benefits or disability payments. As such, they provided the equivalent of the "constituent services" many congressional offices offer today, but on a much more localized, street-by-street, "walk-in" basis. As a consequence, they created loyalty to the Democratic Party as an institution rather than to individual candidates.

These traditional Democratic "machines" declined along with the large factories and ethnic blue-collar neighborhoods of the 1950s and 1960s and no new Democratic-oriented organizations arose to replace them. At the same time, across red state America Republicans were becoming increasingly familiar and active participants in local white working-class community life. As Joe Bageant pointed out in his perceptive book, *Deer Hunting with Jesus*, which describes the working-class town of Winchester, Virginia:

Kerry and the White Working Class

Exit polls typically do not classify respondents by occupation, but they do classify by income as well as education. If one looks specifically at voters who seem to correspond most closely to one's intuitive sense of the heart of the white working class—white voters of moderate income who are not college educated—one finds that these are precisely the voters among whom Democrats did most poorly [in 2004]. For example, among non-college-educated whites with a household income of $30,000–$50,000, [George W.] Bush beat [Democratic candidate John] Kerry by 24 points (62–38); among college-educated whites at the same income level, Kerry managed a 49–49 tie. And among non-college-educated whites with $50,000–$75,000 in household income, Bush beat Kerry by 41 points (70–29), while leading by only 5 points (52–47) among college-educated whites at the same income level. Thus the more voters looked like hard-core members of the white working class, the less likely they were to vote for Kerry in 2004.

Clearly Democrats need to do better among white working-class voters if they are to capitalize on their burgeoning advantage among the constituencies enumerated earlier. And in 2006 and 2008 they were able to do so.

Ruy Teixeira, *"The Evolving Democratic Coalition,"*
in James Cronin, George Ross, and James Scoch, eds.
What's Left of the Left: Democrats and Social Democrats in
Changing Times. *Durham, NC: Duke University Press, 2011.*

Republicans' everyday lives seem naturally woven into the fabric of the community in a way that the everyday lives of the left have not been since the Great Depression ... working-class people encounter Republicans face-to-face at churches, all-you-can-eat spaghetti fund-raisers, fraternal organizations like the Elks club and local small businesses. . . . At the humble level of the small towns, local candidates are raised and groomed for state and national office . . . and it is from these local grassroots GOP business-based cartels that the army of campaign volunteers, political activists and spokesmen springs.

It is critical to recognize that this kind of permanent, on-going, grassroots involvement in community life is profoundly different from the short term, GOTV (Get Out the Vote) "ground game" that Democratic campaigns execute in the months before elections. The typical Democratic ground game is entirely focused on promoting and electing a particular candidate and leaves little or no trace behind after Election Day. Even Obama's vaunted 2008 campaign organization was, in fact, largely passive and almost invisible in between the two subsequent elections of 2010 and 2012. (The campaign's successor organization, Organizing for America, aspires to change this, but is for the moment entirely focused on issues like gun control, immigration and climate change that largely appeal to the liberal base rather than white working-class voters.)

For Democrats to successfully compete with Republicans for the loyalty and support of white working-class voters in the local communities and neighborhoods where they live, a renewed focus on genuine grassroots organization building is simply indispensable. Such organization building will require three things.

First, it will require a commitment to sustained, year-round, door-to-door organizing and relationship building with voters in white working-class communities. New grass-roots Democratic organizations will have to seek to genuinely support and represent white working people in dealing with their day-to-day problems of work and local community life.

Second, the new leadership that these grassroots Democratic community organizations must seek to groom and encourage—whether political candidates or organizational figures—will have to be drawn directly from the communities they will represent and be developed in an authentically democratic and bottom-up way. Democrats cannot copy the cynical Republican model in which professional consultants take a well-funded candidate, give him a flannel shirt to wear, buy him a ranch and then attempt to market him as a cowboy.

Third, the larger Democratic coalition will need to allow these grassroots Democratic organizations in white working-class communities sufficient autonomy and independence to embody and express the distinct ethos of their constituents—an ethos that will combine a "populist" stance on many economic issues with more conservative views on certain—but not all—social issues and a general outlook that reflects a broad cultural traditionalism.

This is a fundamentally different form of organizing than campaign-season ground game work. It would be designed to create permanent and authentic community-level organizations that sincerely represent white working-class voters on an ongoing daily basis and train and support a new generation of Democratic candidates and activists from these communities. It is only genuine grassroots organizations of this kind that can successfully contest the unchallenged position Republicans now enjoy in the daily community life of white working-class America.

A strategy of this kind is inherently a long-term project but even in its very early stages it can materially contribute to changing the attitudes of white working-class voters toward Democrats and progressives and begin to challenge the GOP for their allegiance. Carefully conducted field research by Working America, the 3-million-member community affiliate of the AFL-CIO, has demonstrated that shifts of substantial magnitude in white working-class voting behavior can indeed be achieved by sustained and dedicated door-to-door organizing campaigns.

This is, undeniably, a challenging and difficult strategy, but it is one that offers a plausible path to overcoming the current political stalemate and which is also consistent with the Democratic Party's basic progressive values and its core historic traditions and ethos going back to the New Deal.

> "Conservatives, not progressives, are the ones in need of an electoral strategy to capture this key segment of the electorate."

Setting the Record Straight About the White Working Class

Henry Olsen

Henry Olsen is a senior fellow at the Ethics and Public Policy Center and a former vice president at the American Enterprise Institute. In the following viewpoint, he argues that Democrats actually do better with the white working class than Republicans do. He says the working class is less interested in core Republican messages such as economic advancement and social issues and more interested in a stable, fulfilling life for them and their families. He suggests that Republicans need to rethink their approach to appealing to this demographic.

As you read, consider the following questions:

1. What group does Olsen say Levison curiously overlooks, and what percentage of Americans does this group represent?

2. What messages does Olsen say conservatives use to reach the white working class, and why are these messages not effective?

3. Why does Olsen believe a conservative theory of government will be more appealing to white working-class voters than a progressive one?

One of the most talked about groups in recent elections has been the white working class. Although the group has declined as a share of the nation since World War II, it is still very large at nearly 40 percent of the national electorate. Understanding its views and values is essential to political victory, so it isn't surprising that politicians of all stripes are working hard to gain such an understanding. Andrew Levison's insightful new book *The White Working Class Today: Who They Are, How They Think and How Progressives Can Regain Their Support* tries to provide his fellow progressives with a road map for success with a group Democrats have lost by double digits in recent elections. But the book is more valuable as a source of data and information crucial to strategists of all ideological stripes.

Levison argues that the white working class, contrary to most elite opinions, is not a largely Republican constituency even though Republicans have won the group by double-digit margins in recent elections. He persuasively documents this with opinion surveys that show that these voters are less ideologically conservative than generally recognized. He further shows that many white working-class voters hold contradictory views on most issues, views that blend themes from the right and the left. Accordingly, Levison argues that progressives can target these "moderates" by changing their message from a "we know best" top-down approach to a "you're right, and we're here to help you" bottom-up one. This message can succeed, he says, only by engaging in a serious ground game that literally meets these voters where they live and brings their voices to Washington year-round.

Levison is at his best when describing the attitudes and lives of today's white working class. Census data, for example, demonstrates that white working-class voters earn less and work more in physically demanding jobs than do more educated whites. Working-class men and women are very likely to work in jobs that pay them an average of $21,000 (women) to $31,000 (men) a year. At these wages, it would take two full-time average jobs for a family to earn the median American family income, which perhaps explains why divorce rates are much higher among working-class couples today. A single working-class mother, however, must be under even greater stress. With her meager earnings, she is highly likely to require government aid to pay for medical care and child care, which places the Obama campaign's Julia film (and his electoral success among single women) in its proper context.

The Working-Class Divide: Big Ten Versus SEC

All members of the white working class are not alike, of course, and it is essential to look carefully at their differences. The most important but overlooked traits are religion and region.

There is a very large difference between how southern and non-southern working-class whites vote, one Levison indirectly points toward. He finds, as one might expect, that evangelicals hold more conservative views on most issues than do mainline Protestants, especially those dealing with morality and religion. But on core issues of the size of government or the need for government to help the poor, both branches of Protestantism are largely in agreement, only slightly favoring a smaller government and largely supporting more help for the needy even if it means going further into debt. These findings give Levison hope that progressives can win moderate working-class voters.

However, it is not clear whether Levison has much to worry about. Only 20 percent of evangelicals hold a BA or higher, which means that attitudes specific to evangelicals are more likely to be found among working-class voters. But since evangelicals disproportionally live in or near the South, that means as an electoral matter their views (and their Republican voting patterns) are more of a southern phenomenon than a working class one. Other working-class voters who live in large numbers outside the South are less socially conservative and less focused on religion, and hence are less likely to vote Republican.

A deeper dive into the data sources Levison examines further documents this North-South white working-class divide. White Catholics, a group Levison curiously overlooks, represent about 17 percent of Americans and are a much higher percentage in key midwestern swing states such as Michigan, Iowa, and Wisconsin. The Pew data for Catholics show they are much closer to mainline Protestants than evangelicals on social and economic issues. Since most working-class whites living outside the South and border states are either Catholics or mainline Protestants, one would expect to find that support for Democrats and President Obama is much greater among northern and midwestern working-class whites than among southerners.

That is in fact what the data show. Political scientist Larry Bartels, writing in the respected electoral blog *The Monkey Cage*, finds that President Obama won a majority among non-southern whites in households earning less than $45,000 a year. The president's margin among Levison's core working-class white households—those earning $30,000 a year or less—rises to 55 percent. This figure is supported by exit poll data cited by the *National Journal*'s Ron Brownstein that shows President Obama carried whites without a college degree in Iowa, received 49 percent of their votes in New Hampshire, and 45 percent in Wisconsin. In each state, between 52 and 55 percent of residents are either mainline Protestant or Catholic. Unless Levison hopes for even larger margins, it seems progressives already are attractive to moderate, non-evangelical working-class whites.

The Conservatives' Midwestern Mind

These findings suggest that conservatives, not progressives, are the ones in need of an electoral strategy to capture this key segment of the electorate. The data Levison provides should serve as a starting point for any thoughtful conservative who wants to regain the White House and the Senate.

Conservatives currently rely on three primary messages to reach these non-evangelical white working-class voters. First, delegitimize government by arguing that it is unable to help them get ahead and raise their families whereas the private sector can. Second, argue that when government does act, it too often does so on behalf of undeserving groups, usually illegal immigrants and those who refuse to work. Third, emphasize that conservatives stand on the side of religious liberty and traditional moral values. However, data show that the white working class is not nearly as receptive to these messages as many conservatives hope.

The data show that the white working class does not like government, but has serious questions about whether it can get ahead in today's economy. A 2011 *Washington Post* poll found that 43 percent of whites without college degrees believed that hard work was no longer a guarantee of success. Nearly half thought they did not have the education or skills to compete in today's job market. Attitudes like this strongly suggest that many working-class whites do not instinctively see personal benefits flowing from an untrammeled market.

Many members of the white working class are particularly suspicious of the idea that business leaders and financial experts have their interests at heart. Levison cites data for the white working class from a 2011 Pew survey, "Beyond Red vs.

Blue," that shows that well over half believe that business makes too much profit and that Wall Street does more to hurt than to help the economy. Three-quarters believe that a few large companies hold too much power. These voters do see government as a problem, but they also believe that big government is not the only obstacle in their paths.

Working-class whites also hold more nuanced views on immigration and government's role to provide for the poor than conservatives usually surmise. Levison shows that large majorities of working-class whites think increased immigration is bad for America and favor increased border security rather than immigration reform. But they also strongly oppose free trade agreements. Pew found that the poorest and least educated part of the white working class, labeled "Disaffecteds," think free trade agreements are bad for the United States by a two-to-one margin. These people are being pressed by competition from foreigners at home (immigration) and abroad (free trade), and they don't like it. Conservatives therefore often do not gain the political advantage on immigration that they seek because their free trade views convince working-class whites that conservatives are not on their side.

Working-class white attitudes toward government help for the poor are also nuanced. The Pew study found that half of the white working class believes poor people have hard lives because government benefits don't go far enough and that government should go deeper into debt to help needy Americans. This attitude exists even among usually conservative evangelicals.

Most importantly, delegitimizing government does not cause the white working class to distrust or oppose all government activity, especially those programs that directly impact them. For example, the Pew survey found that 82 percent of "Disaffecteds" oppose cutting Social Security and Medicare to help reduce the federal budget deficit. Only 17 percent favor focusing on cutting major programs to reduce the deficit compared with 59 percent of "Staunch Conservatives."

Conservatives since 1980 have hoped to garner the votes of these economically moderate voters by emphasizing "social issues." It is true that white working-class voters are likely to say that religion is an important part of their lives, and even among Pew's economically distressed "Disaffecteds," 41 percent say they attend religious services at least weekly. But that formal religious commitment does not extend to making social issues a top voting priority.

Levison's data show that the white working class is at best morally moderate. Only 52 percent of whites who have never attended college say that a belief in God is needed to live a moral life. They oppose efforts to get government more involved in protecting traditional morality by a 50–39 percent margin. On homosexuality, 55 percent of whites with a high school degree or less think homosexuality should be accepted by society.

Data for non-evangelical whites with no college experience are not provided, but we should assume given what the data do show about evangelicals generally that these numbers would be even more tilted towards the moral moderation of mainline Protestants and Catholics in this group. Outside of the South and evangelical outposts, then, the stereotypical Reagan Democrat simply doesn't exist.

These data should not come as a surprise to conservatives or the GOP political class. Canadian conservative political wunderkind Patrick Muttart discovered these trends of economic and moral moderation among the Canadian white working class, especially its Catholic members, back in the middle of the last decade. He used that information to propel Prime Minister Stephen Harper to three straight election wins. RealClearPolitics' Sean Trende has noted that Ross Perot in 1992 hiked turnout and got a large vote share in regions of the country dominated by white, non-evangelical working-class voters by running on such an economically and socially moderate platform. This "Perotlandia" is also the part of the country that saw the largest declines in turnout between 2008 and 2012. Nevertheless, I suspect these data remain shocking to most on the right.

Do Conservatives Really Love Raymond?

Conservatives ought to be worried about these findings, but they ought to be more worried about the moral consensus that animates them. Today's conservative movement increasingly emphasizes "getting ahead," "owning your own business," and economic dynamism as essential to the American dream. That's what "you built that" was all about. For whites without any college education, however, these are largely alien concepts.

Levison does a great job in outlining the moral worldview of these voters. They aren't simply not attracted to these goals; they define themselves *in opposition to* these goals.

Levison draws on ethnographic studies to show that for the typical white working-class person, family and stability are more important than career and upward mobility. They saw their middle-class bosses as people who "worried all the time," were "cold and snobbish," and as "arrogant, very arrogant people." They saw their work as "just a job," not a rewarding activity of itself. As befits people who work in teams and do heavy labor, they saw collegiality and practical knowledge to be of greater worth than individual striving and theoretical knowledge. Levison describes this combination as a "distinct combination of viewing work, family, friends, and good character as central values in life while according a much lower value to wealth, achievement, and ambition."

Perhaps this is the conclusion of a progressive seeing the white working-class world through very rose-colored glasses. But why, then, did über-conservative Patrick Muttart find exactly the same values among white workers in his studies?

The GOP and Inequality

As we've seen, this turn toward the welfare state is less a response to growing poverty than to rising insecurity and inequality—and more important, to rising fears of socio-economic stratification, which is the greatest domestic danger facing American society and the real source of conservatives' growing political peril. Inequality and instability only undermine a democratic order when the lower classes feel like there aren't enough ladders leading upward. We don't envy the rich if we think that our kids have a chance of joining them, and we're more likely to accept significant risk if the chances for significant rewards are great as well. This promise of mobility and opportunity has long been the conservative movement's trump card: So long as Americans believe that the poor can rise by their own efforts (and the rich can fall), they're likely to resist efforts to create a European-style nanny state that curtails independence in the name of universal security.

But such mobility is increasingly at risk, as two of the major post-sixties trends in American society—increased meritocracy at the top of society and immigration at the bottom—threaten to freeze the social order in amber.

Ross Douthat and Reihan Salam,
Grand New Party: How Republicans Can Win
the Working Class and Save the American Dream.
New York: Anchor Books, 2009.

Muttart expressed nearly identical sentiments in an extended interview he gave me in 2010. Working-class whites, he told me, are fiscally conservative (low taxes) but economically populist (suspicious of trade, outsourcing, and high finance).

They are culturally orthodox but not generally concerned with social issues because their lives won't change much no matter the outcome. Most importantly, they are modest in their aspirations for themselves. They do not aspire to be "Type A business owners"; they want to go to work, do what's asked of them, not have too much stress in their lives, and spend time with their families. They want structure and stability in their lives so that things they need are taken care of and they don't have to worry.

If Muttart and Levison are correct, and I think they are, then both parties have huge problems attracting these voters. But conservative Republicans have the greater problem because these voters have resisted orthodox Republican economic policies, such as reducing entitlement spending, for decades.

Packers and Lions and Bears: Oh My!

Conservatives who want to regain the presidency cannot ignore these facts. The road to the White House runs through the working-class voter, whether he is white and non-evangelical, as is the case in the Midwest, or Hispanic and marginally Catholic, as is the case in Florida, Colorado, and Nevada. To win their votes, conservative Republicans must first win their trust.

They can do that if they demonstrate that they understand and respect the moral underpinning of working-class life. That moral view places emphasis on hard work and effort and gives respect to those who perform it, regardless of how much money is directly earned. It is one that emphasizes that life is about much more than making money or getting ahead: It's about family, friends, and experiencing the time we have on Earth. Such views cannot be derided as "whiling away the time"; they are central to the working-class world and must be respected.

These views lead to a substantial, but not a dominant, role for government in people's lives. Government should be prepared to help people where they cannot always help themselves, through regulation and redistribution if necessary. Even school vouchers, a conservative Holy Grail, is at heart a redistributive policy that taxes the well-off to give money to the working class to afford a decent education for their kids.

But a conservative theory of government will be substantially different from a progressive one because conservatives understand better than do progressives that working-class voters are makers of their own lives. A conservative approach would emphasize that help would only go to those who help themselves and to those who need it. That means strong work and behavior conditions attached to entitlements and welfare policies, and sharply reducing corporate welfare and tax deductions for the well-to-do. A conservative approach would reduce, where possible, government's monopoly provision of services and let people choose from among providers competing for their favor. A conservative approach would recognize that citizenship means more than voting, and accordingly do more to help people whose lives are unduly stressed because of economic dislocation.

Progressives offer the working class handouts and hands-on regulation of their lives. Libertarian-inspired Republicans offer them a hands-off society that is indifferent to their fate. Conservatives should offer them a new deal. They should offer them what they really want: a hand up.

Periodical and Internet Sources Bibliography

The following articles have been selected to supplement the diverse views presented in this chapter.

Jackie Calmes   "Democrats Try Wooing Ones Who Got Away: White Men," *New York Times*, March 2, 2014.

Dante Chinni   "Politics Counts: If Democrats Motivate Women Voters, Then What?," *Wall Street Journal*, April 11, 2014.

Libby Copeland   "Why Do Women Vote Differently than Men?," *Slate*, January 4, 2012.

Kevin Drum   "Democrats Have Done Virtually Nothing for the Middle Class in 30 Years," *Mother Jones*, March 10, 2014.

Thomas B. Edsall   "How Democrats Can Compete for the White Working Class," *New York Times*, March 11, 2014.

Charles D. Ellison   "Senate Democrats Can't Win Without Black Votes," The Root, January 16, 2014.

Zachary A. Goldfarb   "Democrats Target Unmarried Female Voters," *Washington Post*, April 1, 2014.

David Horsey   "Latinos, Single Women, Young Voters: A Squishy Base for Democrats," *Los Angeles Times*, March 18, 2014.

Frank Newport   "Democrats Racially Diverse; Republicans Mostly White," Gallup, February 8, 2013.

Jonathan Weisman   "Democrats Use Pay Issue in Bid for Women's Vote," *New York Times*, April 8, 2014.

Julian Zelizer   "Why Democrats Need Labor Unions," CNN, July 17, 2012.

OPPOSING
VIEWPOINTS®
SERIES

CHAPTER 3

What Are Controversial Domestic Issues Within the Democratic Party?

Chapter Preface

Education policy has long been a central issue for Democrats. As Matthew Yglesias writes in a February 17, 2014, article at *Slate*, "Democrats have, traditionally, been the party that believes that the quality of educational services provided by the government is very, very, very important." As a result, teachers and their union have tended to align themselves with Democrats. However, in recent years, there has been an important split among Democrats on education policy. Patrick McGuinn in a June 18, 2010, article in *Education Week* describes one faction as supporting "equity" and the other as supporting "accountability."

"Equity" is the more traditional Democratic approach. The group that argues for equity, according to McGuinn, "sees public schools as generally well-performing and attributes poor student performance to the effects of poverty." The goal, then, is to make sure that all students have enough resources. In this view, focusing on student testing is largely beside the point, because the problem is not that teachers are teaching badly, or that schools are not functioning correctly, but rather that schools in poor areas are not being given the resources they need. The problem is with broader public policy and funding, not with individual teachers, schools, or students.

"Accountability," on the other hand, argues that the problem is with individual schools and teachers, who are failing to teach poor and minority students effectively. According to McGuinn:

> In this view, centralized testing and accountability policies are essential to changing the political dynamics around education reform—to breaking a status quo that has prevented schools from taking action to close racial and socioeconomic achieve-

ment gaps despite a large increase in federal and
state education spending over the past forty years.

Again, while the equity view has strong support among many
Democrats and Democratic constituents, the accountability
view has been gaining adherents. Among them is Barack
Obama, who has criticized teachers' unions for opposing initiatives such as testing and charter schools.

In the following chapter, authors examine other controversial domestic policy issues within the Democratic Party, including economic populism, deficits, and domestic spying.

> *"Senators bought into the myth of an omnipotent National Rifle Association. The good news for gun control advocates is that the myth could break in 2016."*

Get Ready for Gun Control as a Wedge Issue in 2016

Nate Cohn

Nate Cohn is a data analyst and journalist who has worked at the New Republic *and the* New York Times. *In the following viewpoint, he argues that the strength of the National Rifle Association (NRA) is exaggerated. Democratic members of Congress who receive poor ratings from the NRA frequently do well in conservative districts, and gun background checks, which the NRA opposes, poll well even in households with NRA membership. Cohn concludes that Democrats could run in favor of gun control in 2016, win, and finally break the myth that the NRA is undefeatable.*

As you read, consider the following questions:

1. According to Cohn, why was NRA spending in the 2012 election largely irrelevant?

2. Why does Bill Nelson's career suggest that the NRA is not that powerful?

3. In what specific geographic areas does Cohn say that gun control could help Democrats?

I'm relatively agnostic about gun control. I'm from the West; I have friends who really like their guns. And I live in the East; I have friends who really hate guns. But it should be troubling to partisans of all stripes when terrible political analysis dictates public policy. Unfortunately, that's exactly what's happened with gun control. This week, the Manchin-Toomey amendment requiring background checks on gun purchases failed in the Senate, in part—perhaps in large part—because senators bought into the myth of an omnipotent National Rifle Association. The good news for gun control advocates is that the myth could break in 2016.

It might seem that only an omnipotent villain could defeat a measure supported by 90 percent of Americans, but don't blame the NRA. Mayor Michael Bloomberg's "Mayors Against Illegal Guns" outspent the NRA on the airwaves by a wide margin. Indeed, Bloomberg spent as much on advertisements over the last month as the NRA spent opposing Democrats in the entire 2012 election cycle. Of course, that doesn't say very much, since the NRA only spent a total of $17 million in 2012's presidential and congressional contests, and the money was spread so thinly across dozens of races that the lobby was largely inconsequential in every contest it entered—and mostly lost.

If it's not the NRA's money, then it must be the ratings. Jonathan Chait recently wrote that, if he were a red state Democrat, he would have voted against background checks to preserve his "A" rating from the NRA. But real senators with low NRA ratings routinely win Senate elections in culturally conservative states. Bill Nelson has an "F" from the NRA and campaigned on gun control in 2000, yet he always outper-

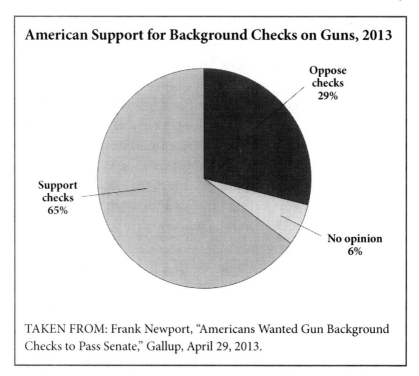

American Support for Background Checks on Guns, 2013

Oppose checks 29%

No opinion 6%

Support checks 65%

TAKEN FROM: Frank Newport, "Americans Wanted Gun Background Checks to Pass Senate," Gallup, April 29, 2013.

forms Democratic presidential candidates in culturally conservative stretches of northern and central Florida. Nelson isn't the only Democrat succeeding in Dixie with an "F." He's joined by Senators Tim Kaine ("F"), Kay Hagan ("F"), Jay Rockefeller ("D"), and Claire McCaskill ("F"). In Ohio, where John Kerry went hunting before the 2004 presidential election, F-rated Sherrod Brown carried much of the southeastern part of the state in 2006 and cleanly won a second term in 2012. Senator Heidi Heitkamp could have peered across North Dakota's eastern border and noticed F-rated Amy Klobuchar winning rural, conservative, western Minnesota with more than 60 percent of the vote.

This isn't to say that there aren't risks to supporting gun control legislation. But background checks? Polls show that every demographic group, including NRA households, support background checks by overwhelming margins. A-rated

Senators Jon Tester, Mark Warner, Pat Toomey, and Joe Manchin all voted for Manchin-Toomey. Mark Pryor's decision to vote against the bill is particularly baffling, since he already had a C-minus rating. I'll be surprised if C-rated Mary Landrieu's 2014 postmortem mentions her vote for Manchin-Toomey, let alone F-rated Kay Hagan's. How many of these voters are supporting Democratic candidates, anyway? My hunch: not many. Red state Democrats take votes that align them with the national party all the time—often taking far bigger risks than supporting popular legislation that's unlikely to spur a great backlash among gun owners.

Even if there were meaningful costs to supporting background checks, the NRA's power is still exaggerated. There's no credible argument that the NRA has a veto over Democratic fortunes outside of the Acela corridor, which is basically what commentators have implied since gun control was blamed for Al Gore's collapse in Appalachia. Not that this really made any sense at the time, since President Bill Clinton signed the Brady Bill and the assault weapons ban before winning reelection with big wins in states like West Virginia. Appalachia's reluctance to return to Democratic presidential candidates since 2000 suggests that these voters have turned toward the GOP for other reasons, or are otherwise lost for good.

The good news for gun control advocates is that the myth could break in 2016. It's easy to envision the next Democratic presidential candidate campaigning on gun control—and winning. Thirteen years ago, Democrats needed rural Ohio, West Virginia, or Missouri to win the presidency. Today, Democratic presidential candidates are less reliant on rural, conservative gun owners than at any time in the history of the party. Democrats win with big margins in cities and suburbs, where support for gun control is an asset, not a hindrance. This is even true in Ohio, where Obama won twice despite losing additional ground in the traditionally Democratic, gun-toting, southeastern part of the state. Now Republicans find themselves in the place that haunted Democrats in the early part of the last decade: To win, Republicans need to reclaim the socially moderate suburbs around Denver, Washington, and Philadelphia, where gun control is a real asset to Democratic candidates.

Obama could have used gun control in the 2012 presidential election, but it wasn't necessary: He had already consolidated the well-educated suburbs by the time of the Aurora movie massacre, which gave him an opening. But if well-educated voters are up for grabs in 2016, or if a more prudent Republican denies Democrats more effective wedge issues like Planned Parenthood, Democrats might instead rely on gun control to consolidate their suburban gains. The 2016 presidential primaries and the possibility that Obama will keep the issue alive suggest that the issue will play a major role in 2016. If Democrats campaign on gun control and win, the myth of the NRA's power may finally fade, allowing innocuous reforms like background checks to become law.

"For two decades, many liberals have
thrived on despising the [National Rifle
Association] and its members. Those
who believe in gun control often hold
enormous prejudice against those who
don't."

Democrats Hurt Their Party by Pushing for Gun Control

Hal Herring

Hal Herring is a journalist who has written for Field & Stream,
High Country News, *and the* Atlantic. *In the following viewpoint, he argues that the Democrats' extreme anti-gun stance
has alienated many gun owners and supporters of the Second
Amendment. Yet, he argues, Republicans are opposed to many of
the core values of gun owners, such as environmental conservation. He concludes that the Democrats should abandon their gun
control agenda so that gun owners can support them against the
Republicans.*

As you read, consider the following questions:

1. According to Dave Workman, what cemented the gun
   voters' dislike of the Democratic Party?

2. Where does Herring say that gun ownership is highest, and why?

3. How does Herring say that the Republican's anti-environmentalist policies will backfire on gun owners?

At this year's annual Gun Rights Policy Conference in September [2008], National Rifle Association [NRA] president Sandy Froman endorsed [Republican candidate] Arizona Sen. John McCain in the upcoming presidential election. This came as no surprise; the Democrats have long been denounced by the NRA as the anti–Second Amendment party—Nanny State know-it-alls, Big-Government gun controllers out of touch with the majority of Americans, yearning to impose their vision on a population that wants none of it.

Move On from Gun Control

In this election, however, it's not that simple. The U.S. is facing a host of challenges, most of them brought on by the antics of a Republican administration that governed as a team of mendacious plunderers, with no regard for the future, or even for the beliefs that their own party once espoused. The Constitution—the very document that guarantees the right to keep and bear arms—has been treated with scorn. The economy, manipulated by the kind of "crony capitalism" we once despised in less enlightened nations, is a shambles, at least for the middle class, and our energy policies are the laughingstock of the developed world. Today's Republicans are not just the party of the Second Amendment; they are also the party of the big energy companies. Is it possible, then, that gun rights advocates might consider voting for someone who is not a Republican?

It's unlikely, unless the Democrats start acknowledging the gun vote and respecting the views of Second Amendment proponents. Gun owners represent at least 4 million of the nation's most dedicated voters. Election after election, they help change the outcome, sometimes electing politicians who are inept, corrupt or unabashed lackeys of corporate interests—people whose only appeal to gun owners is that they promise to leave the Second Amendment alone.

Now, however, the Second Amendment is more resistant to those politicians who might want to mess with it. The Supreme Court's recent *Heller* decision [*District of Columbia v. Heller* (2008)] just declared Washington, D.C.'s restrictive firearms laws unconstitutional, thus weakening the power of state and local politicians to control guns or limit gun ownership. Given that—and given what is at stake in the U.S. today—it may be time for Democratic and Independent voters to simply give up on gun control. We have so many more pressing issues to deal with.

For two decades, many liberals have thrived on despising the NRA and its members. Those who believe in gun control often hold enormous prejudice against those who don't. But there are already reams of laws pertaining to the use, abuse, purchase and sale of firearms. What new regulations would the gun controllers create, and how would they work to address the problem of gun violence? Do they want to prohibit private ownership of firearms altogether? Many would like to ban handguns, without considering just what this would entail, what inequities of power would result, and what new, potentially dangerous powers would have to be awarded to government to accomplish it. Like activists who want to ban pit bulls, the gun control advocates remain relentlessly unspecific about what they hope to achieve. It has become clear, too, that these advocates hold a double standard regarding the U.S. Constitution: The First Amendment is vital to the health of a free nation, as is the Fourth, but the Second is respected only by the un-evolved and the violent. Only the parts of the Constitution that their side respects are valid, in this view.

According to Dave Workman, the senior editor of *Gun Week*, a publication of the Bellevue, Wash.-based Second

Amendment Foundation, "The Clinton-era 'assault weapons ban' was more symbolic than anything else. The reason it was so overwhelmingly supported by the gun control movement was because it represented a federal ban on firearms based on cosmetic circumstances—what they looked like—not on their lethality. It was to condition the public to accept a piecemeal destruction of the Second Amendment."

Republicans Are the NRA Party

Workman believes there was much to learn from the [Bill] Clinton election. "When George H.W. Bush took the gun vote for granted in 1992, most of the gun owners voted for Ross Perot, or else they sat it out," he says. The election of Clinton, though, and what followed, cemented the gun voters' dislike of the Democratic Party. The Brady Law [officially the Brady Handgun Violence Prevention Act] went into effect in 1993, and the "assault weapons ban" passed a year later. That was enough, says Workman, for the gun voters to see "how this was all going. They mobilized and threw out many of the Democrats, costing them control of Congress (in 1994)." The National Rifle Association first endorsed a presidential candidate—Ronald Reagan—in 1980, but gun politics as we know them today were born in 1994.

Since then, the gun vote has gone to the Republicans, and that is not expected to change anytime soon, even with pro-gun Democrats like Montana's Gov. Brian Schweitzer or Sen. Jon Tester gaining prominence. "It is not that the gun vote will not cross party lines," Workman said. "We know that there are a lot of pro-gun Democrats now, and we are not the one-mind, one-thought Neanderthals that many liberals believe us to be. But the Republican Party remains the party of the gun owners, because the most entrenched Democrats are the old-left, dust-gathering anti-gun, anti-liberty politicians, and when the Democrats have a majority, it puts those people in charge."

Guns Endangered

Here in the United States, the Second Amendment has seemingly gone from being a God-given natural right to a privilege that must be defended. Yet the moment anyone dares voice those concerns they are usually met with mockery and dismissed as a bloodthirsty, paranoid freak who is bitterly clinging to their guns even as the mainstream of society passes them by.

Gun rights advocates are thought by the elite controllists to be creatures with the intelligence of a Neanderthal, stubbornly unwilling to accept "commonsense" gun control measures that would allegedly save the lives of countless American children. The mere mention of a "slippery slope," with the Second Amendment itself being the real target, is brushed off as a laughably preposterous conspiracy theory.

The truth—which, as you'll soon see, is not a conspiracy or a theory—is that there are many controllists who want nothing more than to ban guns. They admire Australia and the United Kingdom and Japan and believe that the "civilized" nations of the world have evolved and left America behind. Those countries are the grown-ups while we Americans are the toddlers throwing temper tantrums in a corner.

Glenn Beck, Control:
Exposing the Truth About Guns.
New York: Simon & Schuster, 2013.

Tom Gresham, host of the radio show *Gun Talk*, recognizes that there are dire problems with the Republican Party. Still, he refuses to vote for a Democrat. "I am proud to be a single-issue voter, and I will not cast a vote to strengthen the party of [then House Speaker] Nancy Pelosi. Let's look at what it means when any politician says that it is okay to take away any of the gun rights of a law-abiding citizen. It means that they truly believe that we are too childlike to be trusted with those rights, and it means that their attitude of government is that it will protect us from any and every peril. Tangentially, it also means that they want all the power."

Of his choice of McCain for president, he says: "We all have reservations, I know. But in the long run, I don't really believe that a president can achieve world peace, or solve all of our environmental problems. But I do know that the president can stop the importation of all firearms, can make the cost of a federal firearms license be $10,000, can put OSHA [Occupational Safety and Health Administration] in charge of firearms in the workplace, can empower the EPA [Environmental Protection Agency] to control lead. The president can do these things without any votes, without Congress. And (Obama) is the most anti-gun politician who has ever run for president. Now he is saying that he supports the Second Amendment, but he can support the Second Amendment and still ban guns."

Gresham says the Supreme Court, which could see the appointment of two new, lifelong justices during the next presidential administration, will be the real battleground. "The *Heller* decision is the most important decision on the Second Amendment ever made. And it was 5 to 4. With two justices possibly retiring during this next administration, we cannot afford to have them replaced by justices nominated by Obama, and confirmed by a Democratic Senate."

Gun Rights vs. Social Conservatism

But there are other reasons that the gun vote will go to a Republican. Gun ownership is highest in rural areas, where self-sufficiency is regarded as a virtue, and the Republicans, despite all, have retained the cachet of being the party of bootstrappers. Hunting for meat is a prime example of self-sufficiency, and guns are a part of that sense of self-reliance. One does not give up guns simply because some people use them illegally and create fear and tragedy.

Many Americans value the Second Amendment for a very old reason: as a guarantee, not that tyranny will not happen, but that it can at least be opposed. They believe that the Second Amendment guarantees the existence of all the other amendments, and that, to paraphrase [Renaissance political philosopher] Niccolò Machiavelli, an armed man is a citizen, and an unarmed man is a subject. That doesn't mean that an American who chooses to be unarmed is any less of a citizen, but if we lose the choice to be armed, we have more or less lost the value of our citizenship. Many gun owners find gun control advocates naïve when they argue that guns are useless to fight tyranny in modern times. Today's America is not somehow exempt from the kind of oppression that has at times overtaken every other nation on earth, even our own. Gun control backers act as if we have arrived at the end of history—as if there is far more to fear from an armed populace than there is from anything else that the future may hold.

The gun rights advocates have their own contradictions, though. As a group, they have failed to explain why, if they despise government power, they consistently vote for a political party that has claimed government authority over decisions like abortion rights, religion, and marriage rights. Few gun rights proponents address the attacks on civil rights made by the current Republican administration, or explain why those attacks shouldn't matter when it's time to endorse a Republican candidate for president. Although gun rights and social conservatism may appeal to the same kinds of people, they are actually two opposing ideas. To hold them both smacks of a citizen who does not really value liberty at all, but wants a government empowered to enforce his or her values on everyone else. How is this different from the way gun control advocates want only their values respected?

Single-issue gun rights voters are especially destructive when it comes to environmental issues. Year after year, Republican politicians swear allegiance to the Second Amendment, an act that costs them nothing, but guarantees the gun vote. Then they support measures to exploit, degrade, and even sell off the public lands and waters that hunters and fishermen depend on. Neither the NRA nor the gun voters themselves do anything to protest this. The gun vote has gone to anti-environment politicians for so long now that millions of non-hunting Americans no longer associate hunters with conservation, despite the fact that sportsmen have painstakingly restored wildlife and habitat, rivers and lands, with their gun and ammunition tax dollars, their license fees and waterfowl stamps. This will eventually backfire on gun owners—and on conservationists. In a society increasingly disconnected from nature and hunting, with places to shoot growing increasingly scarce, fewer citizens grow up in a traditional gun culture. That means fewer hunters will fund assets like the federal wildlife refuge system, and fewer shooters will respond to future, inevitable challenges to the Second Amendment.

It is not too late for a new vision, one as unique as the nation itself. If the Democratic Party would recognize the Second Amendment as the Supreme Court has interpreted it in the *Heller* decision, and reassure gun voters that the years of backdoor maneuvers to promote gun control are over, the Republican deadlock on the gun vote could eventually be broken. It seems a small price for the Democrats to pay. All they have to do is recognize the Constitution.

| "The political problems of liberal populism are bad enough. Worse are the actual policies proposed by left-wing populists."

Economic Populism Is a Dead End for Democrats

Jon Cowan and Jim Kessler

Jon Cowan is president of the think tank Third Way; Jim Kessler is senior vice president for policy of Third Way. In the following viewpoint, they argue that liberal economic populism designed to expand the social safety net and tax the rich is not popular outside of very Democratic areas such as New York City and Massachusetts. They add that these policies are economically unfeasible, since the current social safety net is unsustainable even without an expansion. The authors recommend what they say are limited pragmatic economic policies rather than economic populism.

As you read, consider the following questions:

1. What evidence do the authors provide that Bill de Blasio's victory does not have widespread political implications?

2. According to the authors, what tax increases will Senator Warren's policy require?

3. Why do the authors believe the electoral outcome of the tax referendum in Colorado is important?

If you talk to leading progressives these days, you'll be sure to hear this message: The Democratic Party should embrace the economic populism of New York Mayor-elect Bill de Blasio and Massachusetts Sen. Elizabeth Warren. Such economic populism, they argue, should be the guiding star for Democrats heading into 2016. Nothing would be more disastrous for Democrats.

While New Yorkers think of their city as the center of the universe, the last time its mayor won a race for governor or senator—let alone president—was 1869. For the past 144 years, what has happened in the Big Apple stayed in the Big Apple. Some liberals believe Sen. Warren would be the Democratic Party's strongest presidential candidate in 2016. But what works in midnight-blue Massachusetts—a state that has had a Republican senator for a total of 152 weeks since 1979—hasn't sold on a national level since 1960.

The political problems of liberal populism are bad enough. Worse are the actual policies proposed by left-wing populists. The movement relies on a potent "we can have it all" fantasy that goes something like this: If we force the wealthy to pay higher taxes (there are 300,000 tax filers who earn more than $1 million), close a few corporate tax loopholes, and break up some big banks then—presto!—we can pay for, and even expand, existing entitlements. Meanwhile, we can invest more deeply in K–12 education, infrastructure, health research, clean energy and more.

Social Security is exhibit A of this populist political and economic fantasy. A growing cascade of baby boomers will be retiring in the coming years, and the Social Security formula increases their initial benefits faster than inflation. The problem is that since 2010 Social Security payouts to seniors have exceeded payroll taxes collected from workers. This imbalance widens inexorably until it devours the entire Social Security Trust Fund in 2031, according to the Congressional Budget Office. At that point, benefits would have to be slashed by about 23%.

Undeterred by this undebatable solvency crisis, Sen. Warren wants to increase benefits to all seniors, including billionaires, and to pay for them by increasing taxes on working people and their employers. Her approach requires a $750 billion tax hike over the next 10 years that hits mostly millennials and Gen Xers plus another $750 billion tax on the businesses that employ them.

Even more reckless is the populists' staunch refusal to address the coming Medicare crisis. In 2030, a typical couple reaching the eligibility age of 65 will have paid $180,000 in lifetime Medicare taxes but will get back $664,000 in benefits. Given that this disparity will be completely unaffordable, Sen. Warren and her acolytes are irresponsibly pushing off budget decisions that will guarantee huge benefit cuts and further tax hikes for Gen Xers and millennials in a few decades.

As for the promise that unrestrained entitlements won't harm kids and public investments like infrastructure, public schools and college financial aid, haven't we seen this movie before? In the 1960s, the federal government spent $3 on such investments for every $1 on entitlements.

Today, the ratio is flipped. In 10 years, we will spend $5 on the three major entitlement programs (Social Security, Medicare and Medicaid) for every $1 on public investments. And that is without the new expansion of entitlement benefits that the Warren wing of the Democratic Party is proposing. Liberal populists do not even attempt to address this collision course between the Great Society safety net and the New Frontier investments.

On the same day that Bill de Blasio won in New York City, a referendum to raise taxes on high-income Coloradans to fund public education and universal pre-K failed in a landslide. This is the type of state that Democrats captured in 2008 to realign the national electoral map, and they did so through offering a vision of pragmatic progressive government, not fantasy-based blue-state populism. Before Democrats follow Sen. Warren and Mayor-elect de Blasio over the populist cliff, they should consider Colorado as the true 2013 Election Day harbinger of American liberalism.

| *"That's not 'we can have it all,' that's 'let's do the bare minimum so the people of this city can survive.'"*

Third Way Warns Democrats That Running on Popular Economic Positions Would Be 'Disastrous'

Jason Linkins

Jason Linkins is a political reporter for the Huffington Post. *In the following viewpoint, he argues that populist economic positions are actually quite popular and that Democrats who support them should be electorally successful. He also says that populists such as Senator Elizabeth Warren are focused on practical, realistic efforts to preserve Social Security. On the other hand, he says that centrist Democrats have no plan to support Social Security and that centrist arguments are confusing and unhelpful.*

As you read, consider the following questions:

1. What tax specifically does Linkins say Bill de Blasio has proposed?

2. According to Linkins, with what statement does a staggering majority of Democrats agree?

3. What evidence does Linkins provide to suggest that events in New York City are important to the rest of the nation?

Jon Cowan and Jim Kessler of the supposed think tank Third Way have taken to the op-ed pages of the *Wall Street Journal* Tuesday [December 2013] to offer the nation another dose of the hyper-timid incrementalist nonsense for which they're best known. Their case this time involves income inequality, and how trying to ameliorate it is a crazy-dangerous thing for an elected politician to attempt.

Moderate Populist Reforms

At issue here is the fact that New York City Mayor-elect Bill de Blasio and Massachusetts Sen. Elizabeth Warren, both Democrats, recently won elections rather handily—and Warren herself is popular enough nationally to give her "2016 election buzz." These Third Way super-geniuses have assayed the electoral success of these two figures and concluded that their overall message is "bad" for Democrats, because it's based on a "we can have it all fantasy."

Is it, though? De Blasio has proposed, specifically, a modest tax on high-income New York City residents to fund universal pre-K for the whole city (an idea that Gov. Andrew Cuomo will almost certainly kill off in Albany), and more generally wants middle- and working-class residents of New York City to be able to afford to live in New York City. That's not "we can have it all," that's "let's do the bare minimum so the people of this city can survive."

Warren, in general, believes that more can be done to keep consumers from being preyed upon by banks and lenders, and has specifically proposed expanding Social Security. This latter desire is what Cowan and Kessler deem to be the unforgivable sin, despite noting that a "growing cascade of baby boomers will be retiring in the coming years," and that the "problem is that since 2010 Social Security payouts to seniors have exceeded payroll taxes collected from workers." All of which is a pretty good reason to do something like index Social Security benefits to the actual cost of living for seniors, or lift the $113,700 cap on income that is taxed for Social Security— which are basically the modest reforms sought by those who want to "expand Social Security."

But hey, do you want to expand Social Security? According to Cowan and Kessler, you might as well shoot yourself in your very own face, because it's "exhibit A of this populist political and economic fantasy." Per Cowan and Kessler:

> If you talk to leading progressives these days, you'll be sure to hear this message: The Democratic Party should embrace the economic populism of New York Mayor-elect Bill de Blasio and Massachusetts Sen. Elizabeth Warren. Such economic populism, they argue, should be the guiding star for Democrats heading into 2016. Nothing would be more disastrous for Democrats.

Economic Populism Is Popular

How big a disaster would it be for Democrats? Would expanding Social Security be the next Hurricane Katrina, maybe? Well, let's hear what actual Democrats are saying about this stuff.

1. A staggering majority of Democrats agree with the observation that "it's really true that the rich just get richer while the poor get poorer."

2. Among Americans, a clear majority support making no reductions to Social Security or Medicare. About 3 in 10 support only minor changes.

3. The majority of Democrats disagree with the contention that "government regulation of business usually does more harm than good."

4. Esteem for corporate America and Wall Street is falling rather dramatically among Democrats.

5. The coming wave of millennial voters [born since the 1980s] is way, way, way into economic populism. As Peter Beinart reported back in September, "Pew found that two-thirds of millennials favored a bigger government with more services over a cheaper one with fewer services, a margin 25 points above the rest of the population." This population cohort also favored expanding Obamacare [officially known as the Patient Protection and Affordable Care Act], supported labor unions, and was "more willing than their elders to challenge cherished American myths about capitalism and class." The only good news if you hate economic populism is that these same voters "disproportionately favor" the privatization of Social Security. But this is nothing new. As Beinart notes:

> Historically, younger voters have long been more pro–Social Security privatization than older ones, with support dropping as they near retirement age. In fact, when asked if the government should spend more money on Social Security, millennials are significantly more likely than past cohorts of young people to say yes.

So yes, what a disaster this would be for Democrats, if they ran on these wildly popular positions! This is especially bad news for Alaska's Democratic Sen. Mark Begich—no one's idea of a liberal populist firebrand and a lawmaker that's been deemed centrist enough to qualify as a "No Labels Problem Solver." (Cowan is a cofounder of No Labels [a political organization].) Begich is behind the effort to expand Social Security . . . a fact that Cowan and Kessler maybe should have had on hand before they wrote this op-ed.

Having used Google and actual facts and 10 minutes of my time to demolish most of the legs of the Third Way stool, I might as well spend my remaining time hacking the last leg to bits.

> Undeterred by this undebatable solvency crisis, Sen. Warren wants to increase benefits to all seniors, including billionaires, and to pay for them by increasing taxes on working people and their employers.

I don't know, guys, it seems to me that this is actually Warren's offering *in the debate over the Social Security solvency crisis.* One hallmark of particularly weak minds is the tendency to dismiss an actually germane argument about a topic, rather than contend with it.

> Even more reckless is the populists' staunch refusal to address the coming Medicare crisis. In 2030, a typical couple reaching the eligibility age of 65 will have paid $180,000 in lifetime Medicare taxes but will get back $664,000 in benefits. Given that this disparity will be completely unaffordable, Sen. Warren and her acolytes are irresponsibly pushing off budget decisions that will guarantee huge benefit cuts and further tax hikes for Gen Xers and millennials in a few decades.

I think it would be surprising for these Third Way people to learn that Warren *does not actually take the liberal populist position on expanding Medicare.* Warren does not support making substantial cuts to Medicare, but she's rather explicitly stated her opposition to single-payer, which puts her *out of step* with most Massachusetts Democrats. (Again I must ask, is Third Way aware of Google?)

> In 10 years, we will spend $5 on the three major entitlement programs (Social Security, Medicare and Medicaid) for every $1 on public investments. And that is without the new expansion of entitlement benefits that the Warren wing of the Democratic Party is proposing. Liberal populists do not even attempt to address this collision course between the Great Society safety net and the New Frontier investments.

Yeah, I am going to give liberal populists a pass on their failure to address the collision course that vulnerable Americans and their earned-benefit programs are on with this centrist buzz phrase, "New Frontier investments," that Third Way has invented to stand in lieu of something with actual substance.

No Third Way Plan

If you've come this far, you're probably wondering what Third Way's solution to Social Security's "undebatable solvency crisis" is. Well, I'm sorry to report that they don't seem ready to jump into that debate, and have offered nothing of their own. I reckon you'll be waiting a long time, too, given the fact that their wholly fact-averse take on the matter is primarily founded on what amounts to *really funny feelings* they have about the state of the electorate.

In the most comical part of their op-ed, Cowan and Kessler state: "For the past 144 years, what has happened in the Big Apple stayed in the Big Apple." While it's true that Bill de Blasio hasn't exactly become a household name (like Warren has) and New York mayors in particular haven't succeeded in seeking higher office lately (which, oddly enough, hasn't chilled the ardor that Cowan and his "No Labels" organization have manifested for Michael Bloomberg), anyone who knows any-

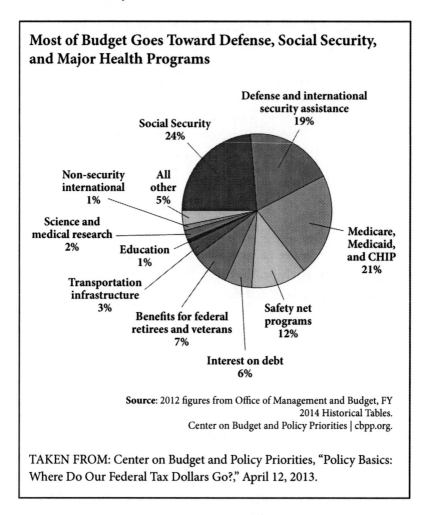

Most of Budget Goes Toward Defense, Social Security, and Major Health Programs

Social Security 24%

Defense and international security assistance 19%

Non-security international 1%

All other 5%

Science and medical research 2%

Education 1%

Transportation infrastructure 3%

Benefits for federal retirees and veterans 7%

Interest on debt 6%

Safety net programs 12%

Medicare, Medicaid, and CHIP 21%

Source: 2012 figures from Office of Management and Budget, FY 2014 Historical Tables.
Center on Budget and Policy Priorities | cbpp.org.

TAKEN FROM: Center on Budget and Policy Priorities, "Policy Basics: Where Do Our Federal Tax Dollars Go?," April 12, 2013.

thing about how cultural trends emerge and spread would find this to be an intellectually untenable thing to say about New York City. It was an attack on New York City, after all, that got one president reelected and the NSA [National Security Agency] all up in our metadata.

But Cowan and Kessler think that the real bellwether, electorally speaking, is a referendum in Colorado:

> On the same day that Bill de Blasio won in New York City, a referendum to raise taxes on high-income Coloradans to fund public education and

universal pre-K failed in a landslide. This is the type
of state that Democrats captured in 2008 to realign
the national electoral map, and they did so through
offering a vision of pragmatic progressive government, not fantasy-based blue-state populism. Before
Democrats follow Sen. Warren and Mayor-elect de
Blasio over the populist cliff, they should consider
Colorado as the true 2013 Election Day harbinger
of American liberalism.

I'm not generally inclined to say that America is two steps
away from becoming de Blasio Nation, but I'm even less inclined to attach too much weight—let alone more weight—to
this referendum and the awesome trend-setting powers of
Colorado politics. (Call me when every state has embraced
Colorado's marijuana laws, and we'll talk.)

Warren obviously favors an expansion of Social Security's
safety net, but her advocacy accomplishes something of secondary importance—it gets the very notion of doing so into
the larger debate. Passing such a law is by no means a done
deal, and I suspect that plenty of Democrats will opt not to
support an expansion. Nevertheless, by shifting that famed
"Overton Window" [the theory that there is a narrow range of
ideas the public will accept] slightly leftward, the effort may
pay off in Social Security not getting scuttled. "I think you've
got to stay with what's possible," Warren herself has said.

I think that Third Way genuinely believes they want to
protect Social Security. But what have they contributed to all
of this, besides criticizing anyone who takes a bold stand?
Well, their basic "doing something substantial for the poor
could really hurt Democrats' reelection chances" stance has
paved the way . . . for President Barack Obama to float
"chained CPI"—a euphemism for making substantial cuts to
Social Security—and make it a legitimate part of the debate.

Wow. Nice work, guys. Say what you want about lawmakers taking a courageous position on Social Security, but how is Third Way's whole "be a gutless simp" approach to the matter working out for everyone else?

> *"The loss of a Democratic opposition to the framework of counterterrorism policy has been one of the most notable aspects of Obama's term in office."*

The NSA Spies and Democrats Look Away

Julian Zelizer

Julian Zelizer is a professor of history and public affairs at Princeton University and the author of Arsenal of Democracy: The Politics of National Security—from World War II to the War on Terrorism. *In the following viewpoint, he argues that during Barack Obama's presidency Democrats and liberals have moved to support an expansion of the national security state. This has included support for National Security Agency spying and on the use of drone strikes, even against American citizens. Zelizer says that this is understandable since partisans usually look to the party leaders to signal policy direction, and Obama has supported spying and national security expansion. However, Zelizer concludes, this lack of opposition may result in bad policy outcomes and may hurt the Democratic Party and America in the long run.*

As you read, consider the following questions:

1. What has been Senator Dianne Feinstein's reaction to revelations about NSA, and how does this compare to other Democratic reactions, according to Zelizer?

2. What example of Republican hypocrisy regarding national security does Zelizer provide?

3. According to Zelizer, how did too much consensus lead to bad decisions in the 1960s?

During the weeks of debates triggered by Edward Snowden and his release of information about a classified National Security Agency [NSA] spying program, the story has moved further and further from the actual surveillance and centered instead on the international cat-and-mouse game to find him.

Liberals Accept Spying

What has been remarkable is how Democrats have expressed little opposition to the surveillance program. Many Democrats have simply remained silent as these revelations have emerged while others, like California Sen. Dianne Feinstein, have openly defended the program.

President Barack Obama, while initially acknowledging the need for a proper balance between civil liberties and national security, has increasingly focused on defending the government and targeting Snowden. When former president George W. Bush offered comments that echoed much of the president's sentiment, some of his supporters couldn't help but cringe as these two one-time adversaries came together on the issue of counterterrorism.

The loss of a Democratic opposition to the framework of counterterrorism policy has been one of the most notable aspects of Obama's term in office. Although Obama ran in 2008 as a candidate who would change the way the government conducted its business and restore a better balance with civil liberties, it has not turned out that way. Obama has barely dismantled any of the Bush programs, and sometimes even expanded their reach in the use of drone strikes and the targeting of American citizens. He has also undertaken an aggressive posture toward those who criticize his program.

Equally notable has been how silent many liberals, who once railed against Bush for similar activities, have become in recent years. Whenever Obama has encountered conservative pushback for minor efforts to change national security operations, there has been little pressure from liberals for him to move in a different direction. If there was any moment when liberals might use a scandal to pressure the president into reforms, this was it. But there is little evidence that this will happen.

Where is the outrage? Where has the Democratic opposition gone? Part of the story simply has to do with political hypocrisy.

Whether or not we like it, partisans tend to be harder on the opposition party than their own. This was clear when Republican opponents of a strong national security system, who gave then president Bill Clinton trouble when he went after homebred white extremists in 1995 and 1996 in the wake of the Oklahoma City bombing [a domestic terrorism bomb attack that killed more than 160 people and injured more than 600], remained silent when President Bush took the same steps against terrorism after 9/11 [referring to the September 11, 2001, terrorist attacks on the United States]—such as in the use of roving wiretaps on cell phones.

Bipartisan Consensus

Democrats have been reluctant to weaken a president who has moved forward on domestic policies they care about by giving him trouble on an issue where their party has traditionally been vulnerable.

The silence on national security is also a product of presidential leadership. One of the functions of a president, as party leader, is to send strong signals about what the party should focus on. When Obama backed away from closing Guantánamo [referring to the Guantánamo Bay detention center] early in his first term, and has been reluctant to do much about the issues of interrogation and aggressive use of American power, he made it much harder for Democratic liberals to do this on their own. By embracing so much of President Bush's national security program, Obama has forged a bipartisan consensus that further marginalized the left and made it harder for them to gain much traction.

Finally, liberals have been split on this issue. The intense animosity toward Bush created the appearance of unanimity, but, in reality, divisions loomed all along. Now that Democrats have been able to debate national security with their own president in the White House, it is clear that many liberals, like Feinstein, believe the government needs to take these steps. Efforts to attack the United States, ranging from the failed plot to bomb the New York City subways to the [2013] Boston bombings, have offered a reminder of the chronic risks the nation faces.

"What do you think would happen if Najibullah Zazi was successful [in 2009]?" Feinstein asked, referring to his effort to bomb a New York subway. "There would be unbridled criticism. Didn't we learn anything? Can't we protect our homeland?"

But Democrats must also remember that too much consensus can lead to bad decisions. During the late 1940s and early 1950s, many liberal Democrats feared being seen as "soft on communism," and allowed reckless and random attacks on Americans accused of allying with the Soviets. This dangerously eroded civil liberties and destroyed many lives.

During the early 1960s, Lyndon Johnson's refusal to listen to the many critics of his Vietnam policies led him deeper and deeper into the quagmire of that war. And during the late 1990s and early 2000s, Democratic fears of being seen as weak on defense led to a ratcheting up of concern about Iraq that helped give Bush the political space he needed to send American troops off to war.

It is possible that further revelations supplied by Snowden to the *Guardian* newspaper's Glenn Greenwald will energize liberal opponents of national security policy and build pressure in Congress for serious investigations and possible reform. But the odds are slim.

It's more likely that most liberal critics of the administration will remain silent and our equivalent of what President Dwight Eisenhower in 1961 called the military-industrial complex—the intricate web connecting defense contractors, the military, members of Congress and the executive branch—will continue to grow.

> "What one sees in this debate is not
> Democrat v. Republican or left v. right.
> One sees authoritarianism v. individu-
> alism . . . insider Washington loyalty v.
> outsider independence."

Support for Domestic Spying Is Not Along Partisan Lines

Glenn Greenwald

Glenn Greenwald is a journalist and lawyer who has written for Salon *and the* Guardian. *He is the author of* No Place to Hide: Edward Snowden, the NSA, and the U.S. Surveillance State. *In the following viewpoint, he argues that it is a myth that Republicans always oppose the president, or that Democrats and Republicans always oppose each other. Rather, he says, on national security issues, many establishment Republicans, such as House Speaker John Boehner, side with President Barack Obama in endorsing spying and the erosion of civil liberties. On the other side, many liberals and conservatives unite in their opposition to spying and what Greenwald says is the undermining of American liberty.*

As you read, consider the following questions:

1. Who is Peter King, and what is his position on NSA spying?

2. According to Greenwald, is the Amash-Conyers bill a "blunt approach"? Why, or why not?

3. Who does Greenwald say is allied against the "decaying establishment leadership"?

One of the worst myths Democratic partisans love to tell themselves—and everyone else—is that the GOP refuses to support President [Barack] Obama no matter what he does. Like its close cousin—the massively deceitful inside-DC grievance that the two parties refuse to cooperate on anything—it's hard to overstate how false this Democratic myth is. When it comes to foreign policy, war, assassinations, drones, surveillance, secrecy, and civil liberties, President Obama's most stalwart, enthusiastic defenders are often found among the most radical precincts of the Republican Party.

Republicans Help Obama

The rabidly pro-war and anti-Muslim GOP former chairman of the House Homeland Security Committee, Peter King, has repeatedly lavished Obama with all sorts of praise and support for his policies in those areas. The Obama White House frequently needs, and receives, large amounts of GOP congressional support to have its measures enacted or bills it dislikes defeated. The Obama DOJ [Department of Justice] often prevails before the US Supreme Court solely because the [conservative] [John] Roberts/[Antonin] Scalia/[Clarence] Thomas faction adopts its view while the [liberal] [Ruth Bader] Ginsburg/[Sonia] Sotomayor/[Stephen] Breyer faction rejects it (as happened in February [2013] when the court, by a 5–4 ruling, dismissed a lawsuit brought by Amnesty [International] and the ACLU [American Civil Liberties Union] which argued that the NSA's [National Security Agency's] domestic warrantless eavesdropping activities violate the Fourth Amendment; the Roberts/Scalia wing accepted the Obama DOJ's argument that the plaintiffs lack standing to sue because the

NSA successfully conceals the identity of which Americans are subjected to the surveillance). As *Wired* put it at the time about that NSA ruling:

> The 5–4 decision by Justice Samuel Alito was a clear victory for the President Barack Obama administration, which like its predecessor, argued that government wiretapping laws cannot be challenged in court.

The extraordinary events that took place in the House of Representatives yesterday [July 24, 2013] are perhaps the most vivid illustration yet of this dynamic, and it independently reveals several other important trends. The House voted on an amendment sponsored by Justin Amash, the young Michigan lawyer elected in 2010 as a [conservative] Tea Party candidate, and co-sponsored by John Conyers, the 24-term senior Democrat on the House Judiciary Committee. The amendment was simple. It would de-fund one single NSA program: the agency's bulk collection of the telephone records of all Americans that we first revealed in this space, back on June 6. It accomplished this "by requiring the FISA Court [Foreign Intelligence Surveillance Court] under Sec. 215 [of the USA PATRIOT Act] to order the production of records that pertain *only to a person under investigation*".

The amendment yesterday was defeated. But it lost by only 12 votes: 205–217. Given that the amendment sought to defund a major domestic surveillance program of the NSA, the very close vote was nothing short of shocking. In fact, in the post-9/11 [referring to the September 11, 2001, terrorist attacks on the United States] world, amendments like this, which directly challenge the surveillance and national security states, almost never get votes at all. That the GOP House leadership was forced to allow it to reach the floor was a sign of how much things have changed over the last seven weeks.

More significant than the closeness of the vote was its breakdown. A majority of House Democrats supported the Amash-Conyers amendment, while a majority of Republicans voted against it. . . .

House Speaker John Boehner saved the Obama White House by voting against it and ensuring that his top leadership whipped against it. As the *New York Times* put it in its account of yesterday's vote:

> Conservative Republicans leery of what they see as Obama administration abuses of power teamed up with liberal Democrats long opposed to intrusive intelligence programs. *The Obama administration made common cause with the House Republican leadership to try to block it.*

In reality, the fate of the amendment was sealed when the Obama White House on Monday night announced its vehement opposition to it, and then sent NSA officials to the House to scare members that barring the NSA from collecting all phone records of all Americans would help the terrorists.

White House Deception

Using Orwellian language so extreme as to be darkly hilarious, this was the first line of the White House's statement opposing the amendment: "In light of the recent unauthorized disclosures, the president has said that he welcomes a debate about how best to simultaneously safeguard both our national security and the privacy of our citizens" (i.e.: We welcome the debate that has been exclusively enabled by that vile traitor [Edward Snowden, who leaked information about American spying], the same debate we've spent years trying to prevent with rampant abuse of our secrecy powers that has kept even the most basic facts about our spying activities concealed from the American people).

The White House then condemned Amash-Conyers this way: "This blunt approach is not the product of an informed, open, or deliberative process." What a multi-level masterpiece of Orwellian political deceit that sentence is. The highly surgical Amash-Conyers amendment—which would eliminate a single, specific NSA program of indiscriminate domestic spying—is a "blunt approach", but the Obama NSA's bulk, indiscriminate collection of all Americans' telephone records is not a "blunt approach". Even worse: Amash-Conyers—a House bill debated in public and then voted on in public—is not an "open or deliberative process", as opposed to the Obama administration's secret spying activities and the secret court that blesses its secret interpretations of law, which is "open and deliberative". That anyone can write a statement like the one that came from the Obama White House without dying of shame, or giggles, is impressive.

Even more notable than the Obama White House's defense of the NSA's bulk domestic spying was the behavior of the House Democratic leadership. Not only did they all vote against de-funding the NSA bulk domestic spying program—that includes liberal icon House Democratic leader Nancy Pelosi, who voted to protect the NSA's program—but Pelosi's deputy, Steny Hoyer, whipped against the bill by channeling the warped language and mentality of [former vice president] Dick Cheney. This is the language the Democratic leadership circulated when telling their members to reject Amash-Conyers:

> "2) Amash-Conyers-Mulvaney-Polis-Massie amendment [a bill supported by House members Amash, Conyers, Mick Mulvaney, Jared Polis, and Thomas Massie]—Bars the NSA and other agencies from using Section 215 of the PATRIOT Act (as codified by Section 501 of FISA) to collect records, including telephone call records, that pertain to persons who *may be in communication with terrorist groups* but are not already subject to an investigation under Section 215."

Remember when Democrats used to object so earnestly when Dick Cheney would scream "The Terrorists!" every time someone tried to rein in the National Security State just a bit and so modestly protect basic civil liberties? How well they have learned: now, a bill to ban the government from collecting the telephone records of *all Americans*, while expressly allowing it to collect the records of anyone for whom there is evidence of wrongdoing, is—in the language of the House Democratic leadership—a bill to protect the terrorists.

Pretend Opposition

None of this should be surprising. Remember, this is the same Nancy Pelosi who spent years during the Bush administration pretending to be a vehement opponent of the illegal Bush NSA warrantless eavesdropping program after it was revealed by the *New York Times*, even though (just as was true of the Bush torture program) she was secretly briefed on it many years earlier when it was first implemented. At the end of June, we published the top secret draft report by the inspector general's office of the NSA that was required to provide a comprehensive history of the NSA warrantless eavesdropping program secretly ordered by Bush in late 2001. That report included this passage:

> "Within the first 30 days of the program, over 190 people were cleared into the program. This number included Senators Robert Graham and Richard Shelby, Congresswoman Nancy Pelosi, President George W. Bush, Vice President Richard Cheney, Counsel to the Vice President David Addington, and Presidential Assistant I. Lewis 'Scooter' Libby."

So the history of Democratic leaders such as Nancy Pelosi isn't one of opposition to mass NSA spying when Bush was in office, only to change positions now that Obama is. The history is of pretend opposition—of deceiving their supporters by feigning opposition—while actually supporting it.

Snowden and NSA Surveillance

Meanwhile, the [Barack Obama] administration found itself unexpectedly on the defensive on another counterterrorism tactic: foreign intelligence–related surveillance of Americans' phone calls and electronic messages. The controversy was touched off by disclosures in mid-June from a former National Security Agency (NSA) contractor, Edward Snowden, in mid-July to the British newspaper the *Guardian* and the *Washington Post.* Documents showed that the super-secret agency collected so-called metadata from telephone companies recording the numbers called by their customers and the date and time of the calls. Snowden, who later fled the United States and gained asylum in Russia, followed with more disclosures detailing the extent of the separate program of monitoring Americans' calls and e-mails with persons abroad. . . .

Even as the Justice Department filed criminal charges against Snowden, his disclosures drew congressional committees, advocacy groups, reporters, and bloggers into efforts to uncover further details about the NSA's electronic surveillance. Lawmakers on both sides of the political aisle voiced concerns about the programs as well as administration officials' lack of candor in detailing the surveillance techniques to Congress. And public opinion appeared to be shifting. An initial poll found Americans evenly divided on whether to approve or disapprove the surveillance program. After more than a month of reporting and debate, a poll by a different organization found nearly three-fourths of those responding thought the surveillance infringed on some Americans' privacy rights.

Kenneth Jost, Obama's Agenda: The Challenges of a Second Term. *Thousand Oaks, CA: CQ Press, 2014.*

But the most notable aspect of yesterday's events was the debate on the House floor. The most vocal defenders of the Obama White House's position were Rep. Mike Rogers, the very hawkish GOP chairman of the House Intelligence Committee [the Permanent Select Committee on Intelligence], and GOP Congresswoman Michele Bachmann. Echoing the Democratic House leadership, Bachmann repeatedly warned that NSA bulk spying was necessary to stop "Islamic jihadists", and she attacked Republicans who supported de-funding for rendering the nation vulnerable to the terrorists.

Meanwhile, Amash led the debate against the NSA program and repeatedly assigned time to many of the House's most iconic liberals to condemn in the harshest terms the NSA program defended by the Obama White House. Conyers repeatedly stood to denounce the NSA program as illegal, unconstitutional and extremist. Manhattan's Jerry Nadler said that "no administration should be permitted to operate beyond the law, as they've been doing". Newly elected Democrat Tulsi Gabbard of Hawaii, an Iraq war combat veteran considered a rising star in her party, said that she could not in good conscience take a single dollar from taxpayers to fund programs that infringe on exactly those constitutional rights our troops (such as herself) have risked their lives for; she told me after the vote, by Twitter direct message, that the "battle [was] lost today but war not over. We will continue to press on this issue."

Liberals and Conservatives Against Obama

In between these denunciations of the Obama NSA from House liberals, some of the most conservative members of the House stood to read from the Fourth Amendment [which protects against unreasonable searches and seizures]. Perhaps the most amazing moment came when GOP Rep. James Sensenbrenner—*the prime author of the PATRIOT Act back in 2001* and a longtime defender of war on terror policies under both Bush and Obama—stood up to say that the NSA's domestic bulk spying far exceeds the bounds of the law he wrote as well as his belief in the proper limits of domestic surveillance, and announced his support for Amash-Conyers. Sensenbrenner was then joined in voting to de-fund the NSA program by House liberals such as Barbara Lee, Rush Holt, James Clyburn, Nydia Velázquez, Alan Grayson, and Keith Ellison.

Meanwhile, in the Senate, Democrat Ron Wyden continues to invoke unusually harsh language to condemn what the NSA is doing under Obama. Here is some of what he said in a speech this week at the Center for American Progress, as reported by the *Hill*:

> Sen. Ron Wyden (D-Ore.) on Tuesday urged the United States to revamp its surveillance laws and practices, warning that the country will 'live to regret it' if it fails to do so.
>
> "'If we do not seize this unique moment in our constitutional history to reform our surveillance laws and practices, we will all live to regret it. . . . The combination of increasingly advanced technology with a breakdown in the checks and balances that limit government action could lead us to a surveillance state that cannot be reversed,' he added. . . .
>
> "The government has essentially kept people in the dark about their broad interpretations of the law, he said. Wyden tells constituents there are two PATRIOT Acts: One they read online at home and 'the secret interpretation of the law that the government is actually relying upon.'
>
> "'If Americans are not able to learn how their government is interpreting and executing the law then we have effectively eliminated the most important bulwark of our democracy,' he said. . . .

"'This means that the government's authority to collect information on law-abiding American citizens is essentially limitless', he said."

Wyden's full speech—in which he makes clear that it is solely the disclosures of the last seven weeks that have enabled this debate and brought about a massive shift in public opinion—is remarkable. . . . That's a senior Democrat and a member of the Senate Intelligence Committee [Senate Select Committee on Intelligence] sounding exactly like Edward Snowden—and the ACLU—in denouncing the abuses of the American surveillance state. Meanwhile, as soon as the House vote was over, Rep. Rush Holt, a longtime Democratic member of the House Intelligence Committee, introduced "The Surveillance State Repeal Act" that would repeal the legislative foundation for this massive spying, including the once-and-now-again-controversial PATRIOT Act, which the Obama administration in 2011 successfully had renewed without a single reform (after Democrat Harry Reid accused opponents of its reform-free renewal of endangering the nation to the terrorists).

Insiders vs. Outsiders

To say that there is a major sea change under way—not just in terms of surveillance policy but broader issues of secrecy, trust in national security institutions, and civil liberties—is to state the obvious. But perhaps the most significant and enduring change will be the erosion of the trite, tired prism of partisan simplicity through which American politics has been understood over the last decade. What one sees in this debate is not Democrat v. Republican or left v. right. One sees authoritarianism v. individualism, fealty to the national security state v. a belief in the need to constrain and check it, insider Washington loyalty v. outsider independence.

That's why the only defenders of the NSA at this point are the decaying establishment leadership of both political parties whose allegiance is to the sprawling permanent power faction in Washington and the private industry that owns and controls it. They're aligned against longtime liberals, the new breed of small government conservatives, the ACLU and other civil liberties groups, many of their own members, and increasingly the American people, who have grown tired of, and immune to, the relentless fearmongering.

The sooner the myth of "intractable partisan warfare" is dispelled, the better. The establishment leadership of the two parties collaborates on far more than they fight. That is a basic truth that needs to be understood. As John Boehner joined with Nancy Peolsi, as Eric Cantor whipped support for the Obama White House, as Michele Bachmann and Peter King stood with Steny Hoyer to attack NSA critics as terrorist-lovers, yesterday was a significant step toward accomplishing that.

> *"For Democrats, entitlements are the fundamental cement that binds their middle-class, blue-collar and low-income constituencies in support of social welfare activism. Weaken this and the coalition of interests that underwrites the liberal state could fall apart."*

Democrats Should Work for Deficit Reduction

Iwan Morgan

Iwan Morgan is a professor of US studies and head of US programs at the Institute of the Americas at University College London, and he is the author of The Age of Deficits: Presidents and Unbalanced Budgets from Jimmy Carter to George W. Bush. *In the following viewpoint, he argues that the Democrats have historically struggled to confront the ballooning cost of entitlements such as Social Security. He argues that failing to deal with entitlements will result in growing deficits, which will constrain spending and hurt the poor and needy who entitlements are intended to help.*

Iwan Morgan, "Obama and the Democrats Need to Confront the Deficit Monster," History News Network, December 7, 2009. Copyright © 2009 by History News Network. All rights reserved. Reproduced by permission.

As you read, consider the following questions:

1. According to Morgan, how did Jimmy Carter split his party?

2. What does Morgan say extinguished the possibility of cooperation on entitlement reform in the Clinton era?

3. What does Morgan say that the Democrats should have done rather than simply pass a health reform bill?

If revenue enhancement is the nettle that Republicans must grasp in the cause of deficit control, entitlement reform has the same significance for Democrats. This has been evident for some time but adjusting the New Deal–Great Society [the New Deal refers to social programs under Franklin Roosevelt and the Great Society to programs under Lyndon Johnson] legacy to the fiscal realities of the twenty-first century poses a huge challenge to the party of Roosevelt. For Democrats, entitlements are the fundamental cement that binds their middle-class, blue-collar and low-income constituencies in support of social welfare activism. Weaken this and the coalition of interests that underwrites the liberal state could fall apart. When making the transition to being the party of deficit control in the late twentieth century, therefore, the Democrats held back from substantive reform of entitlements—even as automatic payments mandated by these programs rose from 47 percent of total federal spending in 1980 to 60.5 percent in 2001.

Avoiding Reform

Jimmy Carter split his party and provoked Edward Kennedy into challenging him for its presidential nomination through his efforts to balance the budget in the battle against inflation instead of pursuing an expansionary fiscal policy to combat unemployment. However, the most fiscally conservative Democratic president since the New Deal ducked the challenge of enhancing Social Security's long-term solvency. True, he supported program amendments in 1977 to deal with an imminent funding shortfall but backed away from the more substantive economies advocated by Health, Education and Welfare Secretary Joseph Califano to run the pension system more tightly without hurting the needier beneficiaries. The threat of a senior citizens' backlash orchestrated by Social Security champions allied to his administration, including his own counselor on aging Nelson Cruikshank, carried more weight with Carter.

In the early 1980s House Democrats led by Speaker Tip O'Neill did much to stall Ronald Reagan's initially successful assault on government by adopting "Save Social Security" as their political mantra. This strategy dissuaded the Republican White House from attempting retrenchment of pensions in the name of deficit reduction and prompted its agreement to establish a bipartisan reform commission, adoption of whose 1983 report ensured Social Security's existence and trust fund solvency into the next century. Nevertheless defense of Social Security against further economies and adjustments became the central plank of Democratic strategy in later Reagan-era negotiations to bring the budget deficit under control. This proved to be smart politics but made for no real progress in resolving deep-seated fiscal problems and preparing for the explosion of pension demand with the retirement of the baby boomer generation.

Clinton and Entitlements

Indicative of Democratic success in portraying the GOP as the enemy of Social Security, the Republicans did not target it for reform in their Contract with America agenda. Once in control of Congress in 1995–96, they focused instead on radical change of Medicare (aimed to encourage seniors to opt for low-cost private health plans) and Medicaid (set for transformation into a block grant). Bill Clinton's high-risk but ulti-

Carter and the Deficit

A conservative Democrat, Carter was the first southerner elected president since Reconstruction ([Lyndon] Johnson won as an incumbent president following Kennedy's assassination), and the last Democratic nominee to win the "solid South" (excepting Virginia). Perhaps lost during the campaign and its aftermath—the definition of the campaign as a repudiation of [Richard] Nixon–[Gerald] Ford and the political resurgence of the South—was the fact that the Jimmy Carter campaign had promised to reduce the deficit by controlling spending:

I had inherited the largest deficit in history—more than $66 billion—and it was important to me to stop the constantly escalating federal expenditures that tended to drive up interest rates and were one of the root causes of inflation and unemployment.

The chief means of addressing the deficit, according to Carter, was eliminating "waste and pork barrel projects in the federal budget."

Scott A. Frisch and Sean Q. Kelly,
Jimmy Carter and the Water Wars: Presidential Influence
and the Politics of Pork. Amherst, NY: Cambria Press, 2008.

mately successful resistance to these GOP initiatives reflected his belief that they threatened the very existence of the liberal state. In his calculus, defense of Medicare was essential to safeguard Medicaid lest diminution of middle-class entitlements made it impossible to protect low-income benefits. In affirmation of his priority to protect the poor, Clinton told his Republican adversaries at their last White House meeting to discuss a budget compromise that would avoid government shutdown, 'I will never sign your Medicaid cuts. I don't care if I go down to five percent in the polls. If you want your budget passed, you're going to have to put someone else in this chair.'

Clinton's triumph over the attempted GOP revolution persuaded Newt Gingrich that more could be achieved through constructive engagement on reform in his second term. Moving towards an unexpected fiscal rapprochement, the president and the speaker agreed to significant entitlement savings in the Balanced Budget Act of 1997. The second phase of their cooperation was to have been a Social Security compromise that would have combined partial privatization of individual accounts with investment in the program trust fund of the bumper federal surpluses that were now expected to stretch far into the future. As a corollary to this, the two leaders also established a national commission on the future of Medicare. However, the Monica Lewinsky scandal [involving Clinton's sexual relationship with an intern] and the consequent Clinton impeachment extinguished all prospect of substantive change owing to their revitalization of political tribalism. Whether Clinton and Gingrich could have persuaded their respective parties to support their entitlement reform initiatives without this development and whether their projected solutions were indeed viable is open to debate. What is not in doubt, however, is that Democrats and Republicans have never again been as close to working together in this common cause.

Health Care

The present imbroglio over the health care bill, particularly its costs and proposed public insurance option, indicates that the divisions of recent history on entitlement reform have intensified rather than diminished. For most Democrats, extension of health insurance to over 30 million Americans unable to afford coverage is a moral obligation and the most significant unfinished business of their party's welfare-state-building history. However, it is difficult to see how this can be achieved without adding to the fiscal deficit, whose inexorable growth will eventually diminish the living standards of many Americans—particularly those whom health care reform is intended to help. The [Barack] Obama administration and its congressional allies might have done better from both a political and policy perspective to devise a comprehensive initiative combining insurance liberalization and robust cost containment—or to organize an independent task force of experts that would have produced recommendations for both ends. As matters now stand, enactment of any health bill can only be the first legislative step towards broader cost control that will require boldness and radicalism, but a White House defeat will diminish its ability to shape this next stage of the agenda. In remarks to a health reform forum in March, Barack Obama acknowledged, "The greatest threat to America's fiscal health ... is the skyrocketing cost of health care." How he deals with this danger will arguably be as important for the historical reputation of his presidency as his foreign policy initiatives to safeguard national security.

> *"I think a deal that cut retirement pro-*
> *grams could be okay in return for*
> *meaningful concessions, like higher*
> *taxes. Since it's not going to happen,*
> *though, Democrats ought to forget*
> *about it for the time being."*

Democrats Should Not Focus on Deficits

Jonathan Chait

Jonathan Chait is a writer and blogger for New York *magazine, a columnist for the* Los Angeles Times, *and the author of* The Big Con: Crackpot Economics and the Fleecing of America. *In the following viewpoint, he argues that the government has in-stituted spending cuts that are reducing the deficit. In addition, Republican refusal to raise taxes means that there is little possi-bility for a deficit compromise at the moment. Thus, he con-cludes, there is no pressing need to focus on deficit reduction in the short term, and there is little chance that such a focus would be successful in any case.*

As you read, consider the following questions:

1. According to Chait, what is Third Way's policy synthesis, and to whom is it designed to appeal?

2. What does Chait say Obama has done to control health care costs?

3. What lesson does immigration reform give about deficit reduction, according to Chait?

Third Way is the think tank—or, at least, what passes for a think tank by contemporary Washington standards—associated with moderate Democrats in the Senate. Of course, there's a place in Washington for a message shop calling itself a think tank that gives moderate Democrats good strategic advice.

Bad Deficit Advice

The trouble is that Third Way gives moderate Democrats terrible strategic advice. Rather than finding a policy synthesis that helps moderate Democrats court red state voters, its policy synthesis is designed to help them court upscale coastal donors. Hence, Third Way urges Democrats to expend their political capital on gun control, which is disproportionately unpopular in red state America, while simultaneously urging them to go to the mat for cutting retirement programs, which are wildly popular everywhere except among the rich. (A helpful explanatory fact: Third Way's codirectors, Jon Cowan and Jim Kessler, are both former gun control activists, and Cowan is a former professional deficit scold.)

Cowan and Kessler's new Third Way memo urging Democrats to cut retirement programs is a fascinating and horrifying encapsulation of current elite sentiment.

Unlike a lot of liberals, I think a deal that cut retirement programs could be okay in return for meaningful concessions, like higher taxes. Since it's not going to happen, though, Democrats ought to forget about it for the time being. Cowan and Kessler allow that "the grand bargain is over," but then, bizarrely, proceed to argue that Democrats should do it anyway.

The most important premise of their argument is that the [Barack] Obama administration has spent too much money. Liberals may complain about austerity, but, they argue, "we haven't had an austerity budget." Cowan and Kessler's evidence for this—that the federal government spent more, on average, during Obama's first term than during George W. Bush's second—demonstrates that they do not grasp what "austerity" means. Austerity means the government reduces its deficit through a combination of spending cuts or tax hikes. Has the government done this? Well, yes, it has. The federal government, after initially implementing a stimulus, has wound down its stimulus, and has since implemented sequestration cuts and tax increases. Deficits are falling very rapidly, and for several years in a row, government cuts have created a net fiscal drag—or, as an economist would call it, "austerity."

Likewise, Obamacare [referring to the Patient Protection and Affordable Care Act, also known as the Affordable Care Act] appears in their piece only as a laudable but costly "new health care entitlement" that "increase[d] spending . . . beyond the breaking point." One correction they propose to this spending binge is to transform the wasteful health care sector, which pays for "quantity of services offered, not the quality." But of course, Obama *did* pass a whole bunch of reforms designed to make health care pay for quality rather than quantity. It's called the Affordable Care Act. And while we won't have any certainty of its effects for many years, the early evidence that the health care–cost curve is bending downward is extremely positive. Reading Third Way's memo, you would conclude that Obamacare did nothing about medical inflation. "Why shouldn't we aggressively solve these problems?" it asks.

The memo does mention the recent slowdown in health care inflation, without mentioning the connection to Obamacare, and then insisting there's "no consensus whatsoever" that the slowdown will last. Well, no. There's no consensus. Many

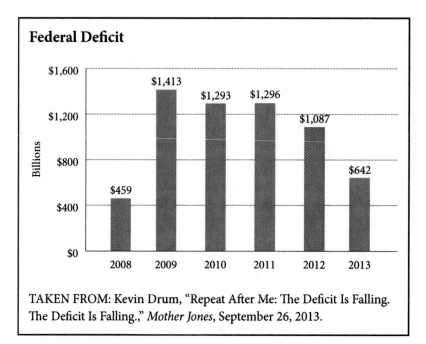

Federal Deficit

TAKEN FROM: Kevin Drum, "Repeat After Me: The Deficit Is Falling. The Deficit Is Falling," *Mother Jones*, September 26, 2013.

health economists think the slowdown will last, but some don't, and nobody is certain, because always in motion is the future.

Still, we could wait a few years and see how this gigantic experiment in bending the cost curve goes, can't we?

Bad Political Advice

No!, insist Cowan and Kessler. Now is the time to act. Why now? Because the politics are perfect:

> the only way entitlements ever get fixed is through divided government. Solutions inevitably include some measure of tax increases and benefit cuts, and no party wants to do that alone.

> Let's face facts. The political roster we have now is as good as it will ever be. We have a Democratic president committed to the safety net, a solid Democratic majority in the Senate with a leader

> committed to the safety net, and a strong minority
> leader in the House also committed to the safety
> net. . . .

What? Have these men not been following the news? There's a Republican-controlled House that does not want to raise taxes. At all. Not even a tiny bit. They don't want to compromise on anything, not even on things, like raising the debt ceiling, that they agree need to happen, let alone on things they don't want to happen. And the current immigration reform negotiations show just how impossible any deal with the House GOP is. You have the entire Republican donor base, backed by a persuasive case for long-term partisan self-interest, and numerous arch-conservative Republicans, like [Florida senator] Marco Rubio and [influential House Republican] Paul Ryan, vocally urging their party to make a deal. I thought an immigration deal would get done, but House Republicans appear to be even more obstinate than I thought, and I already thought they were borderline insane. You're seeing how hard it is to pass immigration reform through the House. A deal with tax increases would be vastly harder.

So given that the deficit is falling really fast, bringing long-term spending and revenue more closely into line might make sense if Democrats could strike a reasonably fair deal, but obviously they can't. The good news is that, the closer Medicare and Social Security get to exhausting their trust funds, the easier it will be to implement tax increases. Americans may not like taxes, but they hate cuts to retirement programs more than anything. So the longer we wait, the easier it gets to secure higher taxes as part of the solution.

Now, here is possibly the weirdest part of their argument, weirder even than their we-don't-follow-the-news argument for getting Republicans to compromise on the budget. They cite this factor as a reason *not* to wait to make a deal:

> Among some elderly advocates, the strategy is to
> delay entitlement fixes for as long as possible, be-

cause the view is that the closer we get to insolvency, the more likely a solution will tilt more toward tax increases rather than benefit cuts. With the elderly and near elderly voting populations representing two of five voters in just over a decade, they are probably right. So, as we are in a pitched international battle for economic livelihood, we can count on future withering tax increases on the middle class to fix these programs.

Bad Tax Advice

"Withering tax increases"? *Withering?* Look, the United States is a very low-tax country, and if we eventually resolve the long-term deficit entirely through taxes, we'll remain a low-tax country. But, even assuming an all-tax-hike solution would be bad because Scandinavia is a socialist hellhole or something, why are we suddenly going to go from a world where Republicans refuse to raise a penny in higher revenue to a world in which tax increases are the entire possible solution? Why not wait until tax hikes are imminent and then strike this balanced deal that replaces some of them with benefit cuts?

If Third Way thinks the problem is simply that the federal government spends too much on retirement programs, and they want Democrats to cut them without insisting on anything in return, then they should say so. That would seem like the only way to make sense of their disparate claims. Otherwise, their argument is pure gibberish.

Periodical and Internet Sources Bibliography

The following articles have been selected to supplement the diverse views presented in this chapter.

Brad Bannon — "Embrace Populism: Democrats Should Push a Message of Economic Security in 2014," *U.S. News & World Report*, March 17, 2014.

Aaron Blake — "Democrats Still Aren't Being Ruthless About Gun Control," *Washington Post*, May 28, 2013.

Tom Curry — "Leading House Democrat Says Job Creation, Not Deficit Cutting, Is Immediate Priority," NBC News, March 17, 2013.

Stephen Dinan and Ben Wolfgang — "Top Democrats Reject Court Ruling over NSA Spying on Americans," *Washington Times*, December 17, 2013.

Richard (RJ) Eskow — "2014 Will Be the Year of 'Economic Populism.' Then What?," *Huffington Post*, December 17, 2013.

Alan Fram — "Gun Control Supporters Struggle to Win Over Some Democrats," *Huffington Post*, March 28, 2013.

James Risen — "Bipartisan Backlash Grows Against Domestic Surveillance," *New York Times*, July 17, 2013.

Arlette Saenz — "Gun Control Advocates, Democratic Lawmakers Make Case for Gun Control," ABC News, September 18, 2013.

Ruy Teixeira and Guy Molyneux — "Everyone Economics: New Data Supports Economic Populism as a Democratic Strategy," *New Republic*, March 10, 2014.

Matthew Yglesias — "Here's How Democrats Want to Cut the Deficit," *Slate*, March 12, 2013.

CHAPTER 4

What Are Controversial Foreign Policy Issues Within the Democratic Party?

Chapter Preface

One major foreign policy debate within the Democratic Party recently involved intervention in Syria. In 2011 Syrian protesters staged uprisings against the dictatorial government of President Bashar al-Assad. The protests turned into a bitter civil war, during the course of which Assad was accused of using chemical weapons against rebel forces. Toward the end of 2013, the Barack Obama administration threatened to respond with military force to punish Assad for the chemical weapons attack.

The threat of military force against Syria was very controversial among Democrats. Lauren Fox in an August 29, 2013, article at CNN noted that some Democrats such as Senator Bob Casey of Pennsylvania were eager for intervention. "Assad has slaughtered more than 100,000 people and stoked sectarianism throughout the region," Casey said. "He has crossed more than a red line and the United States must act in the interest of our national and global security." On the other hand, Chris Murphy, a Democratic senator from Connecticut, opposed the war, arguing that, "before engaging in a military strike against Assad's forces, the United States must understand that this action will likely draw us into a much wider and much longer-term conflict that could mean an even greater loss of life within Syria."

The division over the response to Syria created odd coalitions across partisan lines, according to David A. Fahrenthold and Paul Kane in a September 6, 2013, article in the *Washington Post*. Liberal Democrats opposed to war and conservative Republicans opposed to Obama banded together to create a voting bloc that resisted pressure from both the Democratic administration and House Republican leadership. In the face of this opposition, Obama decided to delay a planned vote on military action in Syria. Instead, the administration reached an agreement with Syria to dismantle its chemical weapons capability, as Barbara Crossette reported in an October 1, 2013, article in the *Nation*. In this case, then, Democratic divisions seem to have forced the Democratic president to alter his foreign policy.

The remainder of this chapter examines other controversies within the Democratic Party on foreign policy, including issues relating to Israel, Iran, and national security.

"Pro-Israel Democrats need to confront
the Jimmy Carter–Jesse Jackson faction's
anti-Israel and occasionally anti-
Semitic animus from the left."

Falling Democratic Support for Israel Is Worrisome and Dangerous

Gil Troy

Gil Troy is a professor of history at McGill University, a research fellow in the Shalom Hartman Institute's Engaging Israel program, and the author of Why I Am a Zionist: Israel, Jewish Identity and the Challenges of Today. *In the following viewpoint, he argues that the Democratic Party is moving away from support for Israel and that this is dangerous both for Israel and for peace and stability in the region. He argues that some Democrats are indifferent to Israel, while others harbor real anti-Israeli sentiment. He says that the mainstream of the party needs to call out the anti-Israeli Democrats and insist that such positions are unwelcome in the party.*

As you read, consider the following questions:

1. According to Troy, what disparity do polls show between Democratic and Republican support for Israel?

2. What are J Street Democrats, according to Troy?

3. What was John Edwards's attitude toward Israel, according to Troy?

When the Democrats restored the party's now traditional affirmation of Jerusalem as Israel's capital, there were so many noes that the move required three attempts to be accepted. Eventually, the plank was pushed through, albeit ham-handedly, to boos from a loud minority. That display of hostility in the Democratic lovefest, as well as the initial desire to drop the Jerusalem plank from the party platform, tells a tale about an internal Democratic debate—and possible shift—that pro-Israel Democrats are desperately trying to cover up.

Anti-Israel Democrats

No matter how many glowing *New York Times* op-eds Haim Saban writes, no matter how many pro-Israel speeches Robert Wexler gives, no matter how many times they channel *Pravda* by hitting the same talking points about Barack Obama's love for Israel, Democrats cannot ignore the elephant—er, over-sized donkey—in the convention hall. Like it or not, the Democratic Party is becoming the home address of anti-Israel forces as well as Israel skeptics. And Democratic support is flagging, with a 15-point gap between Republican support for Israel and Democratic support. I believe strongly that support for Israel should be a bipartisan bedrock—and with more than 70 percent of Americans supporting Israel that foundation remains strong. The new partisan disparity is between an overwhelming 80 percent of Republicans and a still solid 65 percent of Democrats.

I have criticized the Republicans for trying to make supporting Israel a wedge issue through demagoguery. But Democrats should not deny that they are also helping to make Israel a wedge issue by hosting those who are hostile to Israel and then covering it up dishonestly.

As an observer, not a pollster, I perceive four different factions within the Democratic coalition regarding Israel. The largest probably remains the I-love-Israel and I-love-America AIPAC [American Israel Public Affairs Committee] Democrats. These are pro-Israel, pro-Israeli-government liberals, who have no problem being progressive domestically and supporting Israel enthusiastically, especially since 9/11 [referring to the September 11, 2001, terrorist attacks on the United States] and the Palestinian wave of terror reinforced their understandings of the shared values, interests, and needs of the United States and Israel.

Opposition and Indifference

A growing faction, which is probably louder and sounds more influential than it actually is statistically, is the "Tough Love," anti-settlement, J Street Democrats.[1] These people are deeply pro-Israel, but also deeply hostile to the [Prime Minister Benjamin "Bibi"] Netanyahu government, deeply sympathetic to the Palestinians, outraged by the settlements, and convinced that Israel needs to be pressured—not coddled—for there to be peace. Barack Obama has fluctuated between those two positions as president—and there is a disparity of 50 percent to 25 percent in Bibi Netanyahu's favorability ratings among Republicans versus Democrats.

Before his presidency, Obama also flirted with a third faction, which was probably the main source of the booers—enhanced, I would guess, by some J Streeters who are incredibly sensitive to the Muslim-Arab "optics" (meaning how American actions look to the Muslim and Arab world), yet incredibly insensitive to the Jewish-Zionist "optics" (meaning how American actions look to Israel and Israel's supporters). Members of this third Jimmy Carter–Jesse Jackson, Israel-Apartheid, Zionism-racism faction are ardently pro-Palestinian, hostile to Israel—not just its government—and

1. J Street is a liberal advocacy group on Israel policy.

disappointed with Democratic support for Israel. Nevertheless, they are far more disgusted with Republican positions on just about anything, which is what keeps them Democrats.

Finally, and we Israel junkies tend to ignore them, are the "whatever"–John Edwards Democrats. Never forget that many Americans are like [2008 presidential candidate] John Edwards—they just do not care that much about this issue. I am sure that Edwards said the "right" things about Israel so he would get the votes he sought, but he never took leadership, never embraced the Jewish State, and was probably just phoning it in, as my students say.

I will admit, the Jerusalem issue is somewhat of a red herring. It is, like the abortion issue domestically, more symbolic than real—the chances of an American embassy in Jerusalem during the next four years, whoever wins, are about as unlikely as the chances of a reversal of *Roe v. Wade* that would ban abortions. But these symbolic issues count in politics, showing core values, broadcasting an identity, and often indicating where a party is heading.

Under Obama, there has been a drip-drip-drip, a steady draining of general Democratic support for the pro-Israel community. Moreover, Obama's failure to visit Israel after his Cairo speech [to the Arab world in 2009], his testy relationship with Netanyahu (for which both are responsible), his fumbling on the settlement issue (which gave the Palestinians a new excuse to avoid negotiations), the post–[Joe] Biden trip blowup which could have been more astutely handled, his failure just recently to distance himself from General [Martin] Dempsey's insulting remarks about a possible Israeli air strike, as well as this unnecessary Jerusalem platform plank brouhaha, suggest a certain tone-deafness on the Israel file, at best, and a hidden animus, at worst. At a time when those of us who wish to avoid an Iran-Israel war understand that the Israeli government needs reassurance that the United States is completely behind Israel, these kinds of misfires are dangerous.

In the party, J Street Democrats have too often been either a stepping stone for Democrats seeking to distance themselves from their AIPAC comrades or, frankly, a cover for a deeper anti-Israel hostility. Just as in 1991, William F. Buckley confronted Pat Buchanan's anti-Israel and anti-Semitic prejudice on the right, pro-Israel Democrats need to confront the Jimmy Carter–Jesse Jackson faction's anti-Israel and occasionally anti-Semitic animus from the left. If they continue simply uttering denials, offering the same laundry list of Obama's pro-Israel moves, claiming Obama is the *most* pro-Israel president *ever*, they risk losing both their credibility and their dominance in a party that was the party of such champions of Israel as Harry Truman and John Kennedy, Lyndon Johnson and Hubert Humphrey, Bill Clinton and Ted Kennedy, Henry Jackson and Daniel Patrick Moynihan.

"J Street is a heroic attempt to separate the idea of Israel from those who have usurped its government and are now in the process of undermining its very existence."

Falling Support for Israel Will Lead to More Just Policies

Justin Raimondo

Justin Raimondo is the editorial director of Antiwar.com. In the following viewpoint, he praises J Street, an American organization that supports Israel but disagrees with what Raimondo sees as the Israeli government's militant approach to the Palestinians. Raimondo says that J Street has given American Jews an alternate voice in Israel policy, which he says has made the conversation about Israel in the United States more just and more open. He says that J Street also shows that American Jews are not a unified bloc supporting Israel, which he says refutes anti-Semitic myths that suggest that Jews' primary loyalty is to Israel.

As you read, consider the following questions:

1. What is J Street's agenda, according to Raimondo?

2. Why does Ben-Ami refuse to renounce Stephen Walt?

3. Who is Michael Oren, and why does Raimondo think it is best that he did not attend the J Street conference?

For the past few years we've seen a sea change on the question of U.S. relations with Israel, both in the U.S. and in the Jewish state. In America, the idea that our "special relationship" with Tel Aviv dictates a policy of unconditional support has come under attack, not only from critics of Israel but also from some of its most passionate supporters.

A More Reasonable Agenda

In Israel, a wave of right-wing nationalism has installed a government viewed by many as extremist, and roiled relations with Washington. The election of President [Barack] Obama has exacerbated an estrangement that was already developing in George W. Bush's second term. We are witnessing an anti-American trend such as has never before been seen in that country. Obama may be almost as unpopular as the head of Hamas [a Palestinian Islamist organization].

In the U.S., this turn of events has caused many American Jews to have second thoughts, not only about the government of Israel but also its defenders here, who have uncritically supported its policies to the letter. This evolutionary process has produced J Street, a vehicle for American Jews and their friends to advance a more reasonable agenda than that put forth by the traditional pro-Israel lobbying groups.

The occasion of J Street's first national conference, opening this week [in October 2009] in Washington, has put the group at the center of a furious debate, one that often seems obscure to outsiders, i.e., non-Jews. After all, J Street's agenda is no more radical than that advanced by every American president since Jimmy Carter: a two-state solution, peaceful coexistence between Israelis and Arabs, and the tamping down if not the elimination of a conflict that has become a major detriment to U.S. interests in the region. Yet the organization's very existence has caused a brouhaha of major proportions among those for whom Israel is an issue both political and deeply personal.

The reason for this controversy is simple: For many years, the pro-Israel community has conflated support for Israel with support for the policies of its government. Back before the rise to power of such Israeli demagogues as Avigdor Lieberman, this was hardly ever a problem, though there were a few rough patches. The sentiments of the American people were largely, almost reflexively pro-Israel, and the efforts of its government to ensure security in the face of what seemed from a distance to be a uniformly fanatical and violent Palestinian underground evoked much sympathy in the West.

More to the point, American Jews were not noticeably conflicted in their loyalty to the Zionist cause, which had started out as a liberal/progressive crusade for national self-determination. As the power equation changed, however, and the unchallenged military and economic might of the Jewish state made it virtually unassailable by its Arab neighbors, the tide of public—and Jewish—opinion began to turn.

Growing revulsion on the part of many if not most American Jews against the reckless militarism and moral vacuity of Israeli government policies peaked during the recent Gaza "incursion," in which thousands of defenseless Palestinians were killed and maimed—and the government seemed to glory in its own savagery. This, following on the heels of yet another invasion of Lebanon [in 2007], in which civilian targets such as churches, hospitals, and water facilities were bombed, was too much for many of Israel's American supporters to swallow. J Street was born out of a desire to provide an alternative to the view that support for Israel has to mean—by definition—support for the policies of the Israeli government.

This would normally seem like an understandable and mostly positive development, but the word "normally" cannot apply in this instance, because no discussion of Israel is normal, these days. There is so much emotion, mostly on the side of J Street's very vocal critics, that rational discussion is almost impossible.

Demonizing Opposition

This is a deliberate tactic employed by the Israel-is-always-right crowd: By calling the legitimacy of J Street as an organization with a credible agenda into question, right from the start, the Johnnie-one-notes, such as *New Republic* editor Marty Peretz, and the discredited neocons over at the *Weekly Standard*, get to define the terms of the debate. Instead of talking about the rising extremism that is dominating the Israeli body politic and driving an increasing irrational policy of expansionism and perpetual war, we are talking about why J Street has Palestinian contributors and whether the participants in its scheduled "poetry slam" are too pro-Palestinian.

This peculiar atmosphere of inquisitorial hysterics is exemplified by an interview with J Street director Jeremy Ben-Ami conducted by Jeffrey Goldberg in the *Atlantic*. The whole exchange has about it the air of an interrogation: The first question is not a question at all but a demand that Ben-Ami "renounce" Stephen Walt, who has expressed some sympathy for the organization. Ben-Ami, to his credit, demurs, adding:

> "One of the reasons why I won't answer your call to quote-unquote renounce him is that it really smacks of witch-hunts and thought-police. It's not my business to 'renounce.'"

Renounce this, renounce that, and pretty soon you've renounced your way out of existence: Ben-Ami clearly understands this, and is having none of it. He doesn't agree with Walt or his coauthor, John Mearsheimer, who have written a book about the Israel lobby and how it has managed to distort U.S. foreign policy. He makes this unmistakably clear, yet Goldberg is unrelenting. The topic takes up a good third of the interview, going on for paragraphs: "Tell me," Goldberg demands, "about the problem with [Walt's] thesis"!

This whole concept of renunciation of deviationists brings to mind the intellectual and political hysteria that characterized the "Red Decade" of the 1930s, when American leftists were relentlessly hectored by [Joseph] Stalin and his followers to denounce the Trotskyists [those who adhered to the political, economic, and social principles advocated by Communist leader Leon Trotsky] as agents of [Adolf] Hitler and the Mikado [emperor of Japan]. The similarities are structural, and striking: The Communist Party was, in fact, an agent of a foreign power, just as the Old Guard of the Israel lobby is today. As such, it had to hew to a particular line and defend a very specific set of policies, i.e., those formulated by whoever was in power in the Kremlin. This meant that you couldn't just support the cause in general, while dissenting on this or that matter of secondary importance: The defense of the "workers' fatherland" had to be taken up by a united front, and solidarity with the Soviet Union meant, in practice, solidarity with its government. Consequently, the Soviets used the American Communists as their American amen corner. When the Kremlin announced a new policy, the party duly saluted, no questions asked, and energetically began a campaign to sell it to the American people.

The same pattern holds for pro-Israel groups in the U.S., which, unlike the Communists, are not united in a single organization, but which are nonetheless part and parcel of the same movement, one that, historically, has spoken pretty much in a single voice. As Grant F. Smith has shown in his extensive research, the Israeli government directly sponsored and funded earlier efforts to lobby on behalf of Israel, just as Moscow's gold poured into Communist coffers in this country. Any criticism of the Israeli government has been taken, in these circles, as an attack on the Jewish state's very existence. The small—and, now, much smaller—Israeli peace movement was (and is) seen as the enemy, objectively aligned with the Palestinians and their Arab state patrons.

The emergence of J Street as an alternative voice is, in part, a generational shift. The idea that Israel is a refuge for a group of people that is likely to suffer a pogrom at any given moment seems the stuff of fantasy to American Jews who reached voting age in Barack Obama's America. They identify as un-hyphenated Americans and view Israel as a foreign country—one that doesn't always live up to their own moral standards. And they aren't afraid to say so, not just in private, but on the public stage.

As an American president puts pressure on Tel Aviv to moderate its extremist policies, mitigate its militarism, and make some meaningful concessions as the price of our generous support, these American Jews are asking why the Israeli government continues on its suicidal course. The founding of J Street gives them a voice, which is precisely why the dinosaurs of AIPAC [American Israel Public Affairs Committee], the Anti-Defamation League, and the extremists over at the Zionist Organization of America are beside themselves.

Anti-Semitism

The trump card of the Israel lobby has always been the often bogus charge of anti-Semitism. Whenever a critic of the Israeli government dares to write a book, you can bet it will be compared to the [anti-Semitic tract] *The Protocols of the Elders of Zion*—no matter how reasonable, how accommodating to the Zionist project, or how often the author denounces anti-Semitism. A spy is caught handing U.S. secrets to Israel, and within 24 hours a conspiracy theory positing a vast anti-Semitic cabal within the FBI [Federal Bureau of Investigation] is dutifully concocted. A U.S. president asks Tel Aviv to stop building "settlements" on Palestinian land, and he is immediately confronted with the charge of being a "secret Muslim."

The Rise of J Street and the Challenge Posed to AIPAC

The founding of J Street in 2008 fundamentally changed the landscape of the JAPC [Jewish American peace camp]. J Street, a self-proclaimed "pro-peace–pro-Israel" advocacy group, has emerged as a liberal counterweight to the traditionally right-leaning AIPAC [American Israel Public Affairs Committee] and the Conference of Presidents of Major American Jewish Organizations (President's Conference). Founded in April 2008 by former deputy domestic policy advisor to President [Bill] Clinton Jeremy Ben-Ami, who now serves as J Street's executive director, the organization sought to unify the Jewish left wing in America. . . .

Despite years of hard work and dedication, the power and influence yielded by AIPAC and the President's Conference in the United States has long eluded the pro-peace community in America. J Street's founding was a direct response to this ongoing dynamic, the materialization of the notion that to challenge the established right in America, the pro-peace community would have to challenge them at their own game. As of 2011, J Street claimed support from more than 177,000 online supporters, 500 students, and 650 rabbinic cabinet leaders. Further, J Street's second annual national conference, held in February 2011, was attended by more than 2,000 supporters, including 500 students, making the event the third largest gathering of Jews in North America.

Yehuda Magid, "The Jewish American Peace Camp: New Expressions of the Jewish Diaspora," in Galia Golan and Walid Salem, eds. Non-State Actors in the Middle East: Factors for Peace and Democracy. *New York: Routledge, 2014.*

J Street deprives the lobby of its trump card by destroying the fiction that the latter speaks for all Americans of Jewish descent. Heck, I don't believe the Old Guard speaks for even so much as 30 percent, yet it has the loudest voices and the biggest budgets. Well, that won't last, because it cannot last. J Street's bravery in confronting the problem of how Israel survives against all demographic odds is admirable, and one can only hope their brand of cool realism soothes the fevered brow of a movement in crisis.

American Zionism [the desire to work for a Jewish state] is currently undergoing a crisis of conscience, one that pits sympathy for the Jewish state against the historical Jewish sense of social justice. In his deliberately insulting interrogation of Ben-Ami, Goldberg demands to know: "Are you a Zionist?" From what I can tell, what Ben-Ami and a whole new generation of American Jews are saying is the following: Yes to a Jewish homeland, no to a militaristic garrison state. Yes to security, no to "settlements." Yes to [former Israeli prime minister] Yitzhak Rabin, no to [Israeli foreign affairs minister] Avigdor Lieberman. If Goldberg doesn't like it, he can lump it.

There was a contretemps over the invitation to Israeli ambassador Michael Oren to address the J Street conference, and in the end Oren said no. This was made a very big deal of by the Old Guard, which chortled gleefully that the young upstart had been put in its place. But Oren is really doing the new organization a big favor by not coming: His absence gives them the opportunity to distance themselves from the policies of a government that has become increasingly indefensible.

Openness

J Street is a heroic attempt to separate the idea of Israel from those who have usurped its government and are now in the process of undermining its very existence. Oren represents a regime that has arguably committed war crimes and is not only unapologetic but seemingly proud that it has violated moral norms observed by all civilized countries. Oren's presence at a conference dedicated to pushing for peaceful solutions to the Israeli-Palestinian conflict would have added nothing but a note of contention to the event.

The canard that to be an American Jew is to adhere to a dual loyalty was never true and not very convincing, at least to me, yet I get letters all the time from crazies railing on about Zionist control of the U.S. government and how "they" won't let "the truth" come out because "they" control the government, the media, and the weather. I can't communicate how tiresome I find this nonsense; suffice to say that I'm surprised anyone outside of an insane asylum could believe such things. Yet they exist in surprising numbers. Go to any comment thread about Israel, no matter what the context, and you're sure to find this view represented. J Street refutes this canard, because they break the traditional mold of the pro-Israel lobbying community: There is no party line, and certainly not one laid down by Tel Aviv. In short, they are looking out for American interests, in tandem with their support for Israel, and don't see themselves as agents of a foreign power—because they aren't.

No, I don't agree with all of J Street's official positions, but that's not the point. What J Street represents is *glasnost* [Russian for openness] on the foreign policy front, an opening up of the discussion, especially as it pertains to the U.S.-Israeli relationship. That alone is cause for celebration.

| "It is clear that there are majorities—
solid bipartisan majorities—in both
houses for additional pressure on Iran."

Congressional Democrats Rightfully Support Iran Sanctions

Michael Barone

Michael Barone is senior political analyst for the Washington Examiner, *coauthor of* The Almanac of American Politics, *and a contributor to FOX News. In the following viewpoint, he reports that leading Democrats as well as many Republicans support additional sanctions on Iran in order to discourage that country from pursuing a nuclear program. The Barack Obama administration, on the other hand, has reached a deal with Iran and fears new sanctions will undercut the negotiations. Barone argues that more sanctions are needed and that Democrats who oppose the administration on this matter are doing the right thing.*

As you read, consider the following questions:

1. According to Barone, who did the founders say was supposed to make the laws?

Michael Barone, "Congress Is Taking the Lead on Tougher Sanctions for Iran," *Washington Examiner*, December 20, 2013. Copyright © 2013 by Washington Examiner. All rights reserved. Reproduced by permission.

2. What does Barone fear Iran will do in the six months before a final agreement is reached with the United States?

3. How do administration arguments and objectives disconnect on Iran, according to Barone?

Sometimes it seems like things are upside down.

Barack Obama and his Obamacare [referring to the Patient Protection and Affordable Care Act, also known as the Affordable Care Act] administrators are continually making laws, through blogpost (suspending the employer mandate) and bulletin (suspending the individual mandate).

Congress Making Foreign Policy

This [is happening] even though the framers of the Constitution said that it was Congress that would make the laws; the president is just supposed to faithfully execute them.

Meanwhile, members of Congress are, on one issue, moving to make foreign policy—something that for more than a century has been largely left to presidents.

This became apparent last week [in December 2013] when 26 senators, 13 Democrats and 13 Republicans, cosponsored a bill to increase sanctions on Iran.

This is not a new idea. The House voted to increase sanctions last July. And it was sanctions, and the threat of increased sanctions, that surely drove Iran's leaders to the negotiating table where they hammered out an interim agreement with Secretary of State John Kerry in Geneva in November.

That agreement, however, left members of Congress of both parties—and the public—dissatisfied. For the first time, the U.S. recognized, tacitly, Iran's right to continue possessing the centrifuges used to enrich uranium up to the levels needed to produce a nuclear bomb.

It does not take much time or effort to increase the level of enrichment from current to bomb-ready levels.

The agreement leaves a final agreement to be negotiated in six months. But that six-month period only begins when some still unsettled issues are agreed on.

So Iran has more than six months, as things currently stand, to advance its nuclear program—during which time sanctions will be softened and economic pressure on the mullah regime will be reduced.

The public, which tended to give Obama and his foreign policy positive marks during his first term, has tended to oppose Kerry's Iran agreement, polls show. Evidently many ordinary citizens who don't follow issues closely share the fear of many well-informed members of Congress that the United States is giving up too much and gaining too little.

The sponsors of the Senate sanctions legislation include leading Democrats like Foreign Relations Committee chairman Bob Menendez and New York's Chuck Schumer, who has been something of a consigliere for Majority Leader Harry Reid.

Six of the 13 Democratic cosponsors are up for reelection in 2014, as are four of the 13 Republicans (another Republican is retiring).

The top Republican is Illinois's Mark Kirk, a consistent leader on the issue. He is joined with Sens. John McCain, Lindsey Graham and Kelly Ayotte, who work together on many foreign policy issues, and prominent freshmen Marco Rubio and Ted Cruz.

The Will of the People

The Senate bill would impose increased sanctions six months after the Geneva agreement goes into effect unless Iran agreed to certain specified conditions. Top House leaders, including

Iranian Leaders Seen as "Not Serious" About Addressing Nuclear Concerns

Among those who have heard, Iranian leaders are ...

	Nov 2013 %	Dec 2013 %	Change
Serious	33	29	−4
Not serious	60	62	+2
Don't know	7	9	

Survey conducted Dec. 3–8, 2013.
Figures may not add to 100% because of rounding.
Based on those who have heard "a lot" or "a little" about
the agreement on Iran's nuclear program.
Pew Research Center/*USA Today*

TAKEN FROM: Pew Research Center, "Limited Support for Iran Nuclear Agreement," December 9, 2013.

Foreign Affairs Committee chairman Ed Royce and ranking Democrat Eliot Engel, seem ready to pass similar or identical legislation.

Backers argue that it would give administration negotiators leverage on Iran to gain agreement on objectives the president has often said he seeks.

The administration doesn't agree. White House press secretary Jay Carney said flatly last week that the president would veto the bill. Administration lobbyists have been beseeching Democrats not to back it.

Their arguments don't track with their stated objectives. They say they fear Iran will walk out of negotiations if more sanctions are threatened. But tough sanctions are what brought them to the table.

They say new sanctions could be passed later. But the Senate bill doesn't put them into effect until later.

They argue that Iran won't ever agree to end uranium enrichment. But the whole point of sanctions is to get the mullah regime to do something it doesn't want to do. If getting to "yes" were the only objective, we might as well just accept a nuclear-armed Iran.

It's not clear that the sanctions bill will ever get to the floor of the Senate. Even high-caliber sponsors like Menendez and Schumer may be less persuasive with Reid than calls from the White House.

But it is clear that there are majorities—solid bipartisan majorities—in both houses for additional pressure on Iran and for insistence on a final agreement that ends the threat of Iranian nukes rather than one that puts it off for another day.

In this regard, Congress seems to be reflecting the will of the American people. Will the administration listen?

> *"It would be a pity if the bad faith and broken promises were to come from the American side through passage of the Menendez bill."*

New Iran Sanctions? Not Now

Greg Thielmann

Greg Thielmann, a senior fellow of the Arms Control Association, is a former Foreign Service officer who later served on the staff of the Senate Select Committee on Intelligence. In the following viewpoint, he says that the Barack Obama administration has finally negotiated an agreement with Iran that would end the danger of Iran's nuclear program. However, that deal is endangered by Republican senators and some Democrats who want to impose additional sanctions, which would undermine the negotiations and show Iran that America is not dealing in good faith. Thielmann urges Congress to approve the deal with Iran without imposing additional conditions.

As you read, consider the following questions:

1. According to Thielmann, what does Iran have to do in the deal negotiated with the Obama administration?

2. According to Thielmann, what does the United States have to do in exchange for Iranian concessions?

3. What does Thielmann say the United States will do if Iran acts in bad faith?

The international community is finally poised to get a grip on Iran's dangerous nuclear program after more than a decade of trying.

Endangered Breakthrough

This week [in January 2014], Iran is to begin reversing its steady advance toward achieving a capability to rapidly break out of the Nuclear Nonproliferation Treaty [officially known as the Treaty on the Non-Proliferation of Nuclear Weapons] and build the bomb. At least this reversal is likely if the U.S. Senate does not mess things up by voting now to impose new sanctions.

The new sanctions bill (S1881), authored by Sen. Bob Menendez of New Jersey and cosponsored by 58 other senators, including Mark Warner of Virginia, threatens to reopen the deal struck on Nov. 24 [2013] by Iran and six world powers (the United States, Britain, France, Germany, Russia, and China).

This deal calls for Iran, over a six-month period, to get rid of its stockpile of 20 percent–enriched uranium gas—a level close to the weapons-grade material used in the core of nuclear warheads; to freeze its existing stockpile of lower-enriched uranium gas—an enrichment level appropriate for fueling nuclear power reactors; to freeze the number and quality of centrifuges operating to enrich uranium; and to allow an unprecedented level of on-site monitoring by international inspectors.

In exchange, the United States will refund some of Iran's money, now held in escrow, and the six powers will remove sanctions on petrochemicals, precious metal sales, and auto and airplane spare parts. The core sanctions (on oil sales and financial transactions) will not be increased but will remain in place during the six-month first phase, while a comprehensive, final agreement is negotiated.

The Menendez bill establishes new requirements for Iran to fulfill during the initial phase (regarding missiles and terrorist activity) and new preconditions for concluding a final agreement (non-negotiable according to Iran experts), none of which were part of the Nov. 24 agreement.

However disappointing, it is not surprising that a bill President Barack Obama threatens to veto has won support from all but two Republican senators. But it is puzzling that 15 of Menendez's Democratic colleagues have ignored the entreaties of both the White House and the other 10 Democratic chairs of Senate committees to withhold action at this time.

It is also surprising how casually all of the bill's cosponsors dismiss the conclusions of the U.S. intelligence community and academic experts on Iran that passage will make a negotiated agreement less likely.

Bad Faith

The shared understanding among Iran experts is that the new Iranian president won a mandate last June from the Iranian people to negotiate an end to sanctions and isolation, but not at the humiliating price of dismantling Iran's entire uranium enrichment infrastructure. It is also believed that President Hassan Rouhani has been granted only a limited amount of time to achieve results by Supreme Leader Ali Khamenei, who remains deeply distrustful of the United States.

The alternative to a negotiated outcome for preventing a nuclear-armed Iran is war. And people living in the Norfolk area have no illusions about who would bear a disproportionate burden in fighting that war.

Moreover, a U.S. or Israeli military campaign would probably precipitate an Iranian decision to build a bomb (which has not yet been taken) and only postpone rather than prevent Iran from achieving such an objective.

If the Iranians act in bad faith and do not fulfill the detailed commitments they have recently made, it will soon become evident.

In such an event, both the president and Congress have pledged to act quickly to restore the peripheral sanctions that are being suspended and to ramp up the pressure further. It would be a pity if the bad faith and broken promises were to come from the American side through passage of the Menendez bill.

Sen. Tim Kaine, who is chairman of the Foreign Relations Subcommittee on Near Eastern and South and Central Asian Affairs, said Jan. 14 that the U.S. "should not impose additional sanctions against Iran in the midst of this diplomatic negotiation." He's right. Sen. Warner needs to reconsider his position and join in supporting a good-faith diplomatic resolution of the Iran nuclear issue.

Periodical and Internet Sources Bibliography

The following articles have been selected to supplement the diverse views presented in this chapter.

Kristen Soltis Anderson	"Obama Looks Weak Abroad to Those at Home," Daily Beast, February 26, 2014.
Oren Dorell	"Senate GOP Says Democrats Support Iran Sanctions," *USA Today*, January 17, 2014.
Luke Johnson and Jennifer Bendery	"Senate Democrats Back Off Iran Sanctions Vote," *Huffington Post*, January 29, 2014.
Michael Kassen and Lee Rosenberg	"Don't Let Up on Iran," *New York Times*, February 21, 2014.
Josh Kraushaar	"Hagel Pick Pressures Pro-Israel Democrats," *National Journal*, January 6, 2013.
John Podhoretz	"Obama's Failed Foreign Policy Just Another Drag on Democrats," *New York Post*, March 18, 2014.
MJ Rosenberg	"Democrats: Not That into Israel Anymore," *Huffington Post*, April 2, 2013.
Shmuel Rosner	"Israel Factor: Why Is Democratic Support for Israel Weaker than Republican Support?," *Jewish Journal*, January 24, 2013.
Jennifer Rubin	"Democrats' Israel Problem," *Washington Post*, February 27, 2013.
Lydia Saad	"Republicans, Democrats Agree on Top Foreign Policy Goals," Gallup, February 20, 2013.
Sara Sorcher	"Big Democratic Donors Urge Congress to Back Off Iran Sanctions," *National Journal*, February 27, 2014.

For Further Discussion

Chapter 1

1. Jamelle Bouie claims that although most Asian Americans and Hispanic Americans vote for Democrats, these groups may eventually assimilate and vote with the white majority, which may favor Republicans. Do you agree with Bouie's argument? Explain your reasoning.

2. Trymaine Lee argues that restrictions such as voter ID laws will hurt Democrats by suppressing young minority voters. In your opinion, does the study that Lee cites provide sufficient evidence to support his claim? Explain your answer.

3. While a Democratic victory in the House is unlikely, Harry J. Enten contends that such a victory is not impossible. Do you believe a Democratic victory is possible? Provide reasons to support your answer.

Chapter 2

1. Both Shamus Cooke and Chad Stafko assert that labor unions should break away from the Democratic Party. In your view, which author offers more compelling reasons for this conclusion? Explain your answer.

2. Ron Christie argues that neither Democrats nor Republicans are serious about the issues of African American voters. What reasons does Christie give for this argument? Do you agree? Explain.

3. Andrew Levison and Ruy Teixeira maintain that Democrats need the support of white working-class voters to consistently win presidential and congressional elections. Do you agree with the authors' argument? Why, or why not?

Chapter 3

1. Nate Cohn claims that Democrats could campaign on gun control in 2016 and win. Conversely, Hal Herring asserts that Democrats must abandon their gun control agenda. Which author offers the more compelling argument, and why?

2. According to Jon Cowan and Jim Kessler, liberal economic populism is unpopular among most Democrats. Do the authors provide enough evidence to support this claim? Explain your reasoning.

3. Julian Zelizer contends that Democrats and liberals support national security expansion, including spying. Why does Zelizer believe this is true?

Chapter 4

1. Gil Troy argues that some Democrats harbor anti-Israel hostility, and the Democratic Party must confront anti-Israel Democrats. Based on the evidence in the viewpoint, do you agree with Troy? Why, or why not?

2. According to Greg Thielmann, an agreement with Iran to end its nuclear program will be jeopardized if the US Senate votes to impose new sanctions on Iran. In your opinion, should the Senate strike down these new sanctions? Explain your reasoning.

Organizations to Contact

The editors have compiled the following list of organizations concerned with the issues debated in this book. The descriptions are derived from materials provided by the organizations. All have publications or information available for interested readers. The list was compiled on the date of publication of the present volume; the information provided here may change. Be aware that many organizations take several weeks or longer to respond to inquiries, so allow as much time as possible.

American Enterprise Institute (AEI)
1150 Seventeenth Street NW, Washington, DC   20036
(202) 862-5800 • fax: (202) 862-7177
website: www.aei.org

The American Enterprise Institute (AEI) is a research organization dedicated to preserving limited government, private enterprise, and a strong foreign policy and national defense. The institute publishes the magazine the *American*, the current issue of which is available on its website. Also on its website, AEI publishes testimony, commentary, speeches, and articles, including "The Democrats Dilemma," "Democrats and 'Diversity,'" and "Obama's Lyrical Left Struggles with Liberalism."

American National Election Studies (ANES)
Center for Political Studies, PO Box 1248
Ann Arbor, MI   48106-1248
(734) 764-5494 • fax: (734) 764-3341
e-mail: anes@electionstudies.org
website: www.electionstudies.org

The American National Election Studies (ANES) is a joint program of Stanford University and the University of Michigan that is also supported by the National Science Foundation. The mission of ANES is to educate the American public about voting rights and election matters. ANES analyzes voting patterns and issues in the United States and prepares reports and studies for officials, the media, and the general public. Reports and studies, as well as "The ANES Guide to Public Opinion and Electoral Behavior," are available at its website.

Brookings Institution

1775 Massachusetts Avenue NW, Washington, DC   20036
(202) 797-6000 • fax: (202) 797-6004
website: www.brookings.edu

Founded in 1927, the Brookings Institution is a think tank that conducts research and education in foreign policy, economics, government, and the social sciences. The institution analyzes current and emerging issues and produces new ideas that matter for Americans and people worldwide. Its publications include the quarterly *Brookings Review* and periodic policy briefs, while its website offers links to articles and blog posts such as "No Kidding: Republicans, Democrats and Illegal Immigrants" and "Republicans vs. Democrats: Who Has the Answers on Social Mobility?"

Cato Institute

1000 Massachusetts Avenue NW
Washington, DC   20001-5403
(202) 842-0200 • fax: (202) 842-3490
website: www.cato.org

The Cato Institute is a nonprofit research center that approaches policy issues from a libertarian perspective with an emphasis on limited government and individual responsibility. While it analyzes a wide range of issues, the institute has produced several studies and research projects on government and politics in the United States. It has a large number of publications available through its website, including "In Fighting the 'Job Lock,' Democrats Opened a Poverty Trap" and "Democrats Scrub Civil Liberties from Platform."

Center for American Progress (CAP)

1333 H Street NW, 10th Floor, Washington, DC   20005
(202) 682-1611 • fax: (202) 682-1867
website: www.americanprogress.org

The Center for American Progress (CAP) is an independent think tank that works on twenty-first-century challenges such as energy, national security, economic growth and opportunity, immigration, education, and health care. CAP develops new policy ideas, critiques the policies that stem from conservative values, and challenges the media to cover the issues that truly matter. The group also produces numerous articles and policy papers and sponsors *ThinkProgress*, a blog that advances progressive ideas and policies. CAP's recent publications on the topic of the Democratic Party include "Does Obama Have a Problem with His Base?" and "Is Obama the End of Liberalism? Not So Much."

Center for Responsive Politics

1101 Fourteenth Street NW, Suite 1030
Washington, DC   20005-5635
(202) 857-0044 • fax: (202) 857-7809
website: www.opensecrets.org

The Center for Responsive Politics is a nonpartisan, nonprofit research group that tracks money in politics and its effect on elections and public policy. The center conducts computer-based research on campaign finance issues for the news media, academics, activists, and the public at large. Its website contains up-to-date information, charts, and other data on federal elections in the United States. Its Politicians & Elections section contains information on the fund-raising and campaign-financing activities for the Democratic Party for congressional, senatorial, and presidential elections from 2000 to the present.

Democratic National Committee (DNC)

430 South Capitol Street SE, Washington, DC   20003
(202) 863-8000
website: www.democrats.org

The Democratic National Committee (DNC) is a group that governs the Democratic Party. Created during the Democratic National Convention of 1848, DNC plans the party's presidential nominating convention and promotes the Democratic platform, which is the statement of the party's core principles. The committee also raises money, hires staff, and coordinates strategy to support candidates for local, state, and national office. DNC's website offers many resources, including information on immigration reform, education, health care, and national security.

Ethics and Public Policy Center (EPPC)

1730 M Street NW, Suite 910, Washington, DC   20036
(202) 682-1200
website: www.eppc.org

The Ethics and Public Policy Center (EPPC) is a conservative Washington-based advocacy group. The EPPC works to influence public policy and shape public opinion through writing feature articles; publishing its own journal, the *New Atlantis*; and providing legislative testimonies to Congress. The EPPC commonly voices its opinion on matters of public interest, such as health care, the budget and deficit spending, entitlement programs, and immigration reform. The EPPC advocates through feature articles, either as author or as contributor, on issues of national relevance, with titles including "Both Obama and the GOP Badly Damaged" and "The State of the Democrats."

Heritage Foundation

214 Massachusetts Avenue NE, Washington, DC   20002-4999
(202) 546-4400
website: www.heritage.org

The Heritage Foundation is a conservative public policy research institute that supports the principles of free enterprise and limited government. Its many publications include the monthly *Policy Review*, position papers, fact sheets, and reports, including "Democrats Ignore How Climate Change Regulations Hurt Americans" and "Democratic Senator: Obamacare a 'Train Wreck Coming.'"

Third Way

1025 Connecticut Avenue NW, Suite 501
Washington, DC   20036
(202) 384-1700
e-mail: contact@thirdway.org
website: www.thirdway.org

Third Way is a Washington-based centrist think tank that advocates pragmatic solutions and compromise. The organization aims to advance moderate policy and political ideas through progress on social issues such as immigration reform, marriage for same-sex couples, and tighter gun safety laws. Third Way's website includes press releases, archives from its newsletter *Inside Politics*, and reports such as "Millennials— Political Explorers" and "The New Electorate and the Future of the Democratic Party."

21st Century Democrats

2120 L Street NW, Suite 305, Washington, DC   20037
(202) 735-5126
website: www.21stcenturydems.org

21st Century Democrats is an organization that works to train progressives and build a network of populist Democrats. The organization endorses Democratic candidates who represent the tradition of the Democratic Party and who have the potential to move up to higher office. Information on endorsed candidates and various petitions and surveys can be found at the organization's website. 21st Century Democrats instituted AmericasDemocrats.org, its weekly netcast, to deliver in-depth interviews with the nation's top political commentators. Topics discussed on the netcast include the budget, immigration reform, education, foreign policy, the environment, and health care.

Bibliography of Books

Heidi Boghosian   *Spying on Democracy: Government
Surveillance, Corporate Power, and
Public Resistance.* San Francisco, CA:
City Lights Publishers, 2013.

Charles S. Bullock   *Redistricting: The Most Political
III   Activity in America.* Lanham, MD:
Rowman & Littlefield Publishers,
2010.

Robert Busby   *Marketing the Populist Politician: The
Demotic Democrat.* New York:
Palgrave Macmillan, 2009.

Will Clark   *Obama's World: Secrets and
Deceptions.* Diamondhead, MS:
Motivation Basics, 2012.

Jerome R. Corsi   *What Went Wrong?: The Inside Story
of the GOP Debacle of 2012 . . . And
How It Can Be Avoided Next Time.*
Washington, DC: WND Books, 2013.

Jay Cost   *Spoiled Rotten: How the Politics of
Patronage Corrupted the Once Noble
Democratic Party and Now Threatens
the American Republic.* New York:
Broadside Books, 2012.

Charlie Crist   *The Party's Over: How the Extreme
Right Hijacked the GOP and I Became
a Democrat.* New York: Dutton Adult,
2014.

Susan Dunn	*Roosevelt's Purge: How FDR Fought to Change the Democratic Party.* Cambridge, MA: Belknap Press, 2010.
Patrick Fisher	*Demographic Gaps in American Political Behavior.* Boulder, CO: Westview Press, 2014.
Al From	*The New Democrats and the Return to Power.* New York: Palgrave Macmillan, 2013.
Paul Frymer	*Black and Blue: African Americans, the Labor Movement, and the Decline of the Democratic Party.* Princeton, NJ: Princeton University Press, 2008.
Alan Gottlieb and Dave Workman	*These Dogs Don't Hunt: The Democrats' War on Guns.* Bellevue, WA: Merril Press, 2008.
Zoltan L. Hajnal and Taeku Lee	*Why Americans Don't Join the Party: Race, Immigration, and the Failure (of Political Parties) to Engage the Electorate.* Princeton, NJ: Princeton University Press, 2011.
Mark Halperin and John Heilemann	*Double Down: Game Change 2012.* New York: Penguin Press, 2013.
Sanford D. Horwitt	*Feingold: A New Democratic Party.* New York: Simon & Schuster, 2007.
George Lakoff and Elisabeth Wehling	*The Little Blue Book: The Essential Guide to Thinking and Talking Democratic.* New York: Free Press, 2012.

Andrew Levison *The White Working Class Today: Who They Are, How They Think and How Progressives Can Regain Their Support.* Washington, DC: Democratic Strategist Press, 2013.

Anatol Lieven *America Right or Wrong: An Anatomy of American Nationalism.* New York: Oxford University Press, 2012.

Dylan Loewe *Permanently Blue: How Democrats Can End the Republican Party and Rule the Next Generation.* New York: Three Rivers Press, 2010.

Mike Lofgren *The Party Is Over: How Republicans Went Crazy, Democrats Became Useless, and the Middle Class Got Shafted.* New York: Penguin Books, 2013.

George McGovern *What It Means to Be a Democrat.* New York: Blue Rider Press, 2011.

Everett E. Murdock *Obama Won, but Romney Almost Was President: How the Democrats Targeted Electoral College Votes to Win the 2012 Presidential Election.* Los Angeles, CA: H.O.T. Press, 2012.

Jamie Pamelia Pimlott *Women and the Democratic Party: The Evolution of EMILY's List.* Amherst, NY: Cambria Press, 2010.

Larry J. Sabato, ed. *Barack Obama and the New America: The 2012 Election and the Changing Face of Politics.* Lanham, MD: Rowman & Littlefield, 2013.

William A.
Schwab

*Right to DREAM: Immigration
Reform and America's Future.*
Fayetteville, AR: University of
Arkansas Press, 2013.

Jeffrey M.
Stonecash

*Understanding American Political
Parties: Democratic Ideals, Political
Uncertainty, and Strategic Positioning.*
New York: Routledge, 2012.

Karl J. Trautman

*The Underdog in American Politics:
The Democratic Party and Liberal
Values.* New York: Palgrave
Macmillan, 2010.

Michael Walsh

The People v. the Democratic Party.
New York: Encounter Books, 2012.

Tova Andrea
Wang

*The Politics of Voter Suppression:
Defending and Expanding Americans'
Right to Vote.* Ithaca, NY: Cornell
University Press, 2012.

Matthew Yglesias

*Heads in the Sand: How the
Republicans Screw Up Foreign Policy
and Foreign Policy Screws Up the
Democrats.* Hoboken, NJ: John Wiley
& Sons, 2008.

Index

A

Abramowitz, Alan, 75–76

Accountability in education, 139–140

Adaptability, 19, 79–80, 119–120

Addington, David, 177

Affordable Care Act (2010). *See* Patient Protection and Affordable Care Act (PPACA) (2010)

AFL-CIO, 86, 87, 124

African American politicians, 65–66, 104–105
See also Obama, Barack

African American voters
  disenfranchisement methods, 51, 56, 64–65, 69
  economic status, 95–97, 99, 101, 102*t*, 103–104
  education, 99, 103–104
  majority-minority districts, 29, 65–67, 70–71
  Mississippi population, 22–23, 24*t*, 25
  Republican outreach, 99, 103–105
  Texas population, 27
  United States population, 29, 32
  voter ID laws' effects, 46–47, 56
  voting and demographic shifts, 20, 21–27
  voting patterns and participation, 23, 31, 35, 47, 94, 95–97, 97*t*, 100, 101, 103, 105, 109

voting rights, 21, 32, 46–47, 100

Age, voters. *See* Baby boomers; Millennial generation; Senior citizens; Youth vote

Agricultural labor industry, 38

Alabama
  voter demographics, 23
  voting rights history, 64–65, 68

Alaska, 113, 114, 115, 161–162

Alito, Samuel, 174

Amash, Justin, 174–176

American Civil Liberties Union (ACLU), 173, 182

American dream, reconsidered, 130, 133, 134

American Federation of State, County and Municipal Employees (AFSCME), 84, 86

American Israel Public Affairs Committee (AIPAC), 201, 203, 209, 210

American Jews, 204, 205, 206, 209, 210, 211

American South
  Appalachia region, 144
  Democratic presidential candidates, 186
  demographic shifts and voting, 20–27, 120
  historical voting patterns, 20, 21, 22, 186
  proportional representation, 70, 71

E

J